When Horses Speak
and Humans Listen

Andrew-Glyn Smail

Dedication

To our horses, Gulliver, Farinelli, Anaïs and Pip. Thank you for teaching me to listen!

Important Note

What I have learned from horses by listening to them when they have spoken over the years has led me to raise highly critical questions concerning some of the ways we humans interact with them. This criticism I have levelled at such approaches with every intention of exposing the issues involved but with absolutely no desire to judge an individual who pursues any of them.

Ultimately, there is only one human whom any of us have to answer to on behalf of ourselves and the horse(s) in our care and that is the one who stares right back at us when we examine our face in a mirror. When all is said and done, no one else can usurp our place or assume our responsibility for what we choose to do or not to do with the horse(s) in our care.

Possibly as important is the realisation that in the journey that we are each embarked on with a horse, whatever method or approach we pursue may amount to the equivalent of one human's poison being another's sustenance. By way of example, let me mention a development taken from my own journey. In this book I am viciously critical of the "natural horsemanship" approach to training (but not its approach to horse husbandry) as I interpret it here. Yet I will never forget my appreciation when it became the next "big step" forward on the path that I have shared with our horses, for it gave me the wherewithal to feel entirely safe with horses for the very first time in my life. And once I achieved that, a path opened which I would never have believed possible.

Similarly, I am aware that what I am critical of in this book may represent a "big step" forward to another human, perhaps you. If this is the case, please do not interpret my words as a judgment of you, for I have probably been where you are now, relishing that "big step" forward and eagerly seeking the next. Instead, why not simply question what I write but, above all, why not look to your horse to show you the way forward to your next "big step" on the journey that you are taking together?

Contents

FOREWORD

In their own unique way horses "speak" and have been "speaking" to humans for centuries, yet most have chosen not to "listen" to them. Instead, humans have insisted on speaking rather than listening, on telling horses what to do or not to, how to do or not do it and when. And humans have done so not only with their voice but also with an array of metal, leather and plastic devices many of which would not look out of place in a sadomasochistic dungeon or a torture chamber of the Spanish Inquisition. Indeed, the devices which humans use on horses, such as bits, bridles, spurs, metal studs (a.k.a. "horseshoes"), restraints, leads, chains, whips and the like are so harsh as to have inspired an entire niche form of sexual BDSM practice known as "ponyplay". And these humans do this, not because they are desperate to eke out a living, but largely for pleasure, status, profit or a combination of such pursuits. I used to be just such a human until ten years ago I chose to listen to horses speak.

Over the years I have been a close observer and student of horses, our own and others, in various parts of the world. During the past decade, in particular, horses have been instrumental in fundamentally changing my life and outlook on it. Much of that journey has been documented in the Horses and Humans blog (which you can find at www.horsesandhumans.com/blog) and a series of three books based on it entitled *In Search of the Master Who Dances with Horses: Challenge*, *Growth* and *Being* (more information available here: www.horsesandhumans.com/mainsite/-books.htm – without the hyphen). In the course of this process I have published some of my developing insights into horses and their interaction with humans and members of their own species in the form of discussion papers and/or blog posts. They constitute the basis for this book, into which I have gathered and edited them to reflect the fruits of my experiential learning with and from the horses along with feedback provided by other humans on a similar journey. The resultant articles have acquired a form which will hopefully contribute to our understanding of these magnificent creatures and the capacity they have to help us become more sensitive, caring, nurturing, reliable and dependable friends to them, ourselves, the earth and all to whom it is home.

Available in print and all the most common e-book formats, this book has been arranged largely in the order in which I wrote the articles. As such, a discerning reader may note, as I have on reworking them, that I seem to have moved from more of an intellectual grasp of the changes that needed to occur within me and in my interaction with horses towards an experiential understanding of those changes as they began and continued to occur. Although I have edited what I wrote at the time, I have not made any attempt to hide this evolution, as I feel that this may be more appropriate for any reader who, like me, has started out with little more than a conviction that they want a meaningful, mutually beneficial and joyful relationship with an equine friend rather than a dutiful creature who does their bidding instantaneously and unquestio-ningly.

In my case the inspiration came in the form of the mutually trusting relationship between Klaus Ferdinand Hempfling and his loyal chestnut gelding, Janosch, on display in the DVD originally published in German in the early 1990s and entitled *Dancing with Horses* when it was subsequently issued in English at the turn of the century, a video which I only saw for the first time in 2007. At the time I had largely abandoned attempts to do anything with horses, because I simply could not see the point of making such a splendid creature do or not do as I required. Then I saw that living example of a mutually trusting relationship between horse and human exhibited in Klaus and Janosch, and I immediately knew that it was precisely what I could treasure having with a horse if only I knew how to achieve it. And so I took the first step towards a horse-friendly way of being with horses and the learning curve that I came to experience in the ten years since then is largely reflected in this collection of articles.

The articles

The first two articles were inspired by Hempfling's book, *Dancing with Horses*, which contains a few gems of wisdom that I immediately recognised as such. Given the limited development of my new, horse-friendly approach at the time, however, my understanding of them was more of an intellectual acknowledgement of the direction in which I should be heading and the articles read as such. Yet my experience with horses since then has largely confirmed the conclusions that I drew after rereading the first two chapters of Hempfling's book.

Dancing with Horses: The Shimmering Star

This article sets out a number of fundamental prerequisites for any meaningful relationship and interaction with horses. When I first read them in *Dancing with Horses*, I recall that I was really excited because they invited me to embark on a very different path to the horse from the *cul de sac* I had previously travelled on and had abandoned. I was called upon to feel, to have fun, to enter the ongoing moment of being with the horse in which the journey becomes the destination. A decade later I can confirm that the horses have shown me the truth of what was then little more than an intellectual acknowledgement.

Dancing with Horses: Communication, Dominance and Trust

Although again largely inspired by *Dancing with Horses*, the book rather than the DVD, by the time I wrote this article I had also come to be inspired by *Empowered Horses*, a book written by another German, this one a woman called Imke Spilker. While this article contains much that I subsequently came to reject, such as Hempfling's insistence on "dominance" and "leadership", it does highlight an element which is absolutely indispensable if a human ever wishes to relate to a horse as a fellow sentient being, namely, the need for self-development within the human, both physical and "spiritual". Here the latter term is not used to refer to some pie-in-the-sky religious belief system but rather the development of the awareness and consciousness which the human will require if they ever wish to truly enter the realm of horses. Again, this was more of an intellectual exercise at the time, which has since been confirmed to a large extent through experiential learning with horses.

On Top of the Mountain: Achieving a Magical Connection with Your Horse

This article was inspired by a series of two videos entitled *Immediate Connecting with Horses*, Parts 1 and 2, published by Klaus Ferdinand Hempfling on YouTube. Again, it also draws on Imke Spilker's *Empowered Horses* as well as the writings of a horseman who has played a huge role in helping me find my direction with horses, Michael Bevilacqua from Canada, in particular his book, *Beyond the Dream Horse*. Essentially, this article deals with the prerequisites for establishing an energetical (which I referred to as "magical" at the time) connection with a horse. Intellectually, I knew what needed to happen and the article reflects this but all my experimentation was getting me nowhere with our horses. The more I tried, the further off the connection seemed. More water needed to flow under the bridge before I stopped trying and expecting or hoping, and instead started to feel and sense at gut level without expectation. It was then that the magic happened.

Yielding to Pressure: The Reality of the Myth

Over the years I have studied various aspects of the nature of the horse as part of formal studies, such as those for Equine Touch bodywork and saddle-fitting. Knowledge of equine physiology and anatomy, amongst other things, I have supplemented with observations made while watching and interacting with horses in a variety of environments in various countries around the world. This is the first article I wrote which actually draws on this and it was prompted by an observation made by the well-known ethologist,

4

Lucy Rees, to the effect that it is not in the nature of a horse to yield to physical pressure but rather to resist it, something which I had already observed with our own horses. And yet yielding to physical pressure is at the heart of horse training as part of both the conventional and "natural horsemanship" approaches. The article challenges this notion and also covers other forms of "pressure".

Horse Training: Living the Dream or Creating an Illusion?

There is this virtually unquestioned assumption in the equestrian world that, if you have a horse, they need to be trained. After all, what else do you do with a horse apart from ride them and ensure that they are physically healthy? Even those of us who are committed to living the dream of a new, horse-friendly way of relating to horses have been and/or are still tempted to assume that the most effective way of doing so is to train them to come to us, walk and trot with us at liberty and do anything else which could show the "close" relationship between horse and human in a YouTube video, as though it is possible to teach friendship, understanding, trust and unconditional love. This article examines the question of whether training enables us to live our dream of the type of relationship that we are seeking with our horse or whether it merely creates the illusion of doing so, and if it is merely the illusion, why this is the case.

Contemplations on Riding a Horse

These contemplations comprise a series of three relatively brief articles covering issues that arose while preparing to ride my mare, Pip, for the very first time after she had not had a human on her back for several years and I had effectively been out of the saddle for ten years or more.

The first of these articles, *Riding What?*, considers what is required in relation to the horse before contemplating riding.

The second article, *To Ride or Not to Ride? This is the Question*, considers the pros and cons of riding in relation to the horse, covering their physical and mental condition, tack and natural collection or self-carriage.

The third article shows the evolution of my approach from the second article in its title: *To Ride or Not to Ride: Is This Really the Question?* Various commentators reveal their approach to the question of riding or not but ultimately it is my horse's "comment" which makes the greatest impression. This is followed by one of the most profound revelations which had been staring me in the face for some time but for which I required the assistance of a horseman on the other side of the world to finally acknowledge.

It's about the Horse, Isn't it?

It is very easy to be attracted by a particular approach to horses, whether Western, classical, "natural horsemanship" or anything else, so much so that we become not only enthusiasts but downright uncompromising disciples. The approach assumes such an overriding importance that it is very easy to lose sight of the creature that is its subject, namely, the horse. And when we finally realise that it is about the horse, what implications does this have for us and the creature in front of us?

Lessons Taught Me by My Horse

Five years after Pip came into my life, I looked back on our experience together and reviewed what I had learnt from her. These lessons are profound and have made all the difference in the ongoing development of our relationship with each other, as well as between other horses and myself.

Horses and the Myth of Leadership

The "natural horsemanship" movement has made and is still making a major impact on the horse world. Central to its approach to interaction with horses and training them is its insistence on a leadership model which has the human acting as the leader and the horse the follower without any choice in the matter. Said to be derived from horses in the wild, this model has been and still is being embraced by other sectors of the horse world very often without question. Yet how reliable is this leadership model? This article argues that in relation to horses the concept of leadership is a myth and explains why.

From Natural Horsemanship to Holistic Horse-Humanship
Drawing together some of the threads dealt with in previous articles, this is a no-holds-barred rejection of the "natural horsemanship" approach to training, which in many instances is proving to be more harmful to horses than the abuse which it claims to abolish. It is simultaneously a passionate plea for a new paradigm in our approach to the species, one which I have called holistic horse humanship for the reasons outlined in this article.

Horses and the Art of Followership
This is one of the most radical insights that horses have shared with me. For some years the idea had suggested itself to me but, being the bossy little man I can sometimes be tempted to become, it was not one that I entertained readily. After all, following is a concept which suggests a lack of initiative and a passivity which reeks of submissiveness, is it not? Perhaps it is … until in the course of a brief but intense light-bulb moment I was able to view all of the scattered signs together and connect the dots. It was then that I fully realised how powerful true followership is and how potentially subversive and transformative it could be if transposed into the human situation.

The Power of Being with Horses
I shall always be grateful to horses for showing me the power of being, because it has changed not only my relationship with them but also my life and outlook on it. And ultimately, it is so easy to gain access to this power. There are times when I regret that I did not do so earlier in my life but then I recall how blessed I am to have discovered the power of being before it ends and I am profoundly thankful to the horses for this.

Acknowledgements

Firstly, I must acknowledge the contribution of the horses, in particular, those in our immediate care: Gulliver, the wise, patient, strong-willed survivor who is the equine epitome of dignity and perseverance, Farinelli, the frequently misunderstood juvenile who has rediscovered the joys of youth as he enters his twilight years, Anaïs, my muse when I really needed one and the horse who showed me graphically more than any other that there is no need to resort to restraints and whips for fear she will rear majestically but threateningly, because she understands clarity and kindness, luxuriating in these qualities like a big, purring pussycat, and Pip, who has challenged me to dig deep within myself for the strength to resist yielding to the easy temptation to exploit her initial submissiveness and who has taught me better than any other horse that one of the paths to human self-development lies not in equine aided, facilitated, guided or whatever but rather in caring for horses without expectation. Words fall short in any attempt to express my appreciation for what you and the other horses who have passed through my life in the past ten years have taught me. You spoke, I listened and we are still painting magic as a result.

Finally, I would like to express my appreciation for a few of the humans who have been exceedingly instrumental in helping me learn from all the horses who have patiently put up with me in the past decade. First and foremost amongst them is Klaus Ferdinand Hempfling for the inspiration that set me off on my journey with horses, for helping me realise that change had to occur within myself rather than the horses, for emphasising the need for body and spiritual awareness on the part of the human in this process, for pointing to the general direction in which I might find assistance to achieve both, and for forcing me – unintentionally though it may have been – to follow the path to the horse without leaning on him as a crutch. Then there is the gentle, unassuming horseman from Canada, Michael Bevilacqua, who taught me that in our relations with horses "understanding and trust have nothing to do with training" and that everything we do with or for them should follow from unconditional love.

I would also like to thank all readers who took the time to read and comment on the original versions of these articles when they were first published as discussion papers or blog posts. Your comments have played a key role in helping me understand the horses that have spoken to me. In some cases you have also been instrumental in causing me to revise what I had written.

These acknowledgements would be incomplete without special mention of the woman who has chosen to be my lover, partner, wife and best friend for close to 35 years. Victorine van Rossem. Without our ongoing reflection on and discussion – sometimes heated and robust – of what we experience with horses, ours and others, and what we have learned from, with and about them, it would have been far more difficult to make sense of it all. Thank you!

Andrew-Glyn Smail
Andalusia, Spain
Autumn, 2017

DANCING WITH HORSES: THE SHIMMERING STAR

(Reflections on rereading Klaus Ferdinand Hempfling's *Dancing with Horses*. All references are to the Trafalgar Square Publishing edition of 2001. See the Bibliography for more details.)

It is easy to gate-crash *Dancing with Horses*, the book, by bypassing the "accompaniment" which precedes the text proper but you will do yourself a disservice if you do, because it is crucial to understanding an approach to horses in general and riding them in particular which is more empathetic towards the species and more empowering for both horses and humans than the bum-back interface which normally serves as the basis of the relationship between the two. I am referring to the approach adopted by Klaus Ferdinand Hempfling to horse-riding in general and his elucidation of it in *Dancing with Horses*, in particular. This accompaniment tells the story of a noble caballero, who while lying on his deathbed at the age of 96, laments the misfortune of his impending demise with tears in his eyes. Listening to him, his nephew is puzzled, pointing out that "this time comes for every man" and that his uncle has had a "long, rich, blessed life". The old man concurs but immediately confesses that "it was only about a week ago that I first realised what it means to truly ride a horse".

To Hempfling riding a horse represents the summit of a unique cross-species experience, the vast bulk of which involves extensive interaction between horse and human on the ground as they establish and develop a close relationship with each other, and the intuitive and physical prowess that riding and the lead-up to it demand. This is an approach which is also reflected in the number of pages devoted to riding in *Dancing with Horses* and their position in the book, namely, the last 62 of a total of 204 pages (30%). The contrast is even greater in Hempfling's much later book, *The Horse Seeks*

Me, which only devotes the last 45 of a total of 343 pages (13%) to riding.

The theme of *Dancing with Horses*, Hempfling tells us, is "collected riding on a loose rein", a "reconciliation of opposites" which is "probably as old as riding itself" but which "has managed to stay virtually unknown" (p. 13). Even though "The Art of Body Language" is cited as the book's subtitle on its cover, it is "Collected Riding on a Loose Rein" which features as its subtitle on the title page of Kristina McCormack's fine English translation (and which is the English translation of the subtitle of the original German edition). Together these opposites – "the collected horse, a being bursting with pride and power, quiet and yet animated, schooled and strengthened by man solely to carry man upon his back", and "the loose reins a symbol of willingness, a symbol of partnership, trust and harmonious friendship" (p. 13) – seem "a bit like a star, shimmering in the night sky, so very far away, unreachable and other worldly, almost unreal" (p. 15), and the world's current cream of dressage superstars can testify to this as they so ably demonstrate at each outing in the globe's premier competitive events.

If the goal is so apparently unattainable that our world and Olympic champions cannot even attain it, why then should any human even contemplate the journey? Hempfling likens it to *From the Earth to the Moon*, a science fiction novel written by the French writer, Jules Verne, in 1865 (the book is – accorded the title of a 1902 black-and-white film – loosely based on the novel in the translation of *Dancing with Horses*). The idea of landing on the moon was a dream and realising it involved a long, arduous task which demanded enormous effort and eventually only came true 204 years later. Even then only two humans set foot on the moon and, although others followed in their footsteps, ultimately only a tiny clutch of humans were involved. Yet humanity as a whole has benefited from the experience, Hempfling argues: "Only a very few people actually set foot on the moon but their path to the goal brought us all an infinite amount of new knowledge that today is seen as more important and useful than actually reaching the intended goal" (p. 15). And it is in this that we may find the answer to our question as to why any human should ever contemplate the journey. As Hempfling puts it, "our shining star" of collected riding on a loose rein "is far off and beautiful, and even to set off on the journey towards it is an act of great consequence" (p. 15).

This produces one of three principles which Hempfling articulates to guide our actions. In a world in which "guiding principles seem to have little meaning … and where only the winner is important" (p. 17), he sets out the following three guiding principles. First of all, whatever we do must always be fun. This principle is important enough to be printed in a bold font: ***"what we do is only worthwhile if it is done in a spirit of joy and adventure, for ourselves and for our horses"***. The statement is so trite that it is ridiculously easy to gloss over it, yet it is so demanding as to be potentially life-changing. Consider for a moment just what is required in order to do everything with our horses in "a spirit of joy and adventure" (p. 18) . We are being called upon to be happy, not just to feel it on the odd occasion but to be it as long as we are with horses. In this sense, if we want to be with horses, we are being challenged to do what it takes to ensure that we are happy. Put another way, if you are not happy, stay away from horses. It is bad enough that you have to put up with your own unhappiness. Why saddle horses with it as well?

The second principle which Hempfling enunciates is this. If the path we are following is appropriate, what we do with horses will be beautiful. The bold print puts it this way: ***"everything we do will always be beautiful, from the first lesson on"***. This is the sense we get when "everything is magic".

The third guiding principle is arguably the most challenging yet simultaneously the most liberating. Allowing it to guide us will also enable us to act in accordance with the first two principles. The bold print in the book (p. 19) says it all:

> **If the path we have embarked upon is good, and we have conquered the need to be bigger and better than anyone else, that is marvellous! Then there is no more stress, everything we do is always fun, is always beautiful and the goal has become irrelevant. It will never be reached**

anyway, even by the most talented (see *An Accompaniment*).

And here we come full circle to where we started: the old man who has finally realised (just before his death) what it means to ride a horse has been reaching his goal every day while on the journey towards doing so. In short, the path has become the goal.

Oh alright, so Hempfling has got all the answers then, has he? So tell me how I am going to do this then. I have a full-time job, then there are the kids and a partner who need to be fed and the house has to be cleaned, then there are the school … the medical … and the …. And I have a mare that is full on and goes over the edge every time she comes within sniffing distance of a hunk in the herd but I have no time available other than to throw a saddle on her a few times a week to go out for a ride.

Reading between the lines, this is an easy one to answer but a difficult answer to put into practice: find the horse a new home or radically change my life. If it is not fair on me to relate to my horse in this fashion, it is definitely not fair on my horse either. Neither of us deserve this.

However, if throwing out my partner and kids is an option or, better still, if I am willing to go in search of a solution which enables me to keep them while starting on my journey to that distant, shimmering star, then Hempfling has an invitation for me:

> Let us put ambition to one side and begin to listen and to see. Above all, let us begin to "feel"! The ability to feel is a gift from God to each of us. Let us begin to feel ourselves and to understand our horses. Let us commit ourselves to this journey which is attended by unending successes and constant joy, this journey that makes it possible for us to stop putting off enjoyment of today's work until tomorrow, or the day after, or until we have achieved some goal of questionable worth. Let us begin this journey that allows us *to live fully in the here and now*, just as our horses actually teach us to do (p. 19 – emphasis added).

DANCING WITH HORSES: COMMUNICATION, DOMINANCE AND TRUST

(Reflections on rereading Klaus Ferdinand Hempfling's *Dancing with Horses*. All references are to the Trafalgar Square Publishing edition of 2001. See the Bibliography for more details.)

In Chapter 2 of *Dancing with Horses* Klaus Ferdinand Hempfling (Hempfling) defines the essence of riding a horse as "communication and balance". The corollary to this is that any form of interaction with a horse other than riding will at the very least necessitate communication, if not balance as well. He then goes on to stipulate two prerequisites for such communication. To many who seek a humane form of interaction with a horse, one of these is self-evident: trust. If you are to communicate with your horse, they need to trust you implicitly. The other prerequisite which Hempfling postulates is almost guaranteed to raise the hackles on the necks of the same category of humans: dominance. This is partly because the concept of dominance is often accorded the negative connotations of its linguistic cousin, "domination", and partly because the latter is so typical of modern conventional approaches to horsemanship, including those relying on refined forms of pressure and release.

Let us briefly examine these three concepts in the order in which they are mentioned in the book (communication, dominance and trust) and determine whether there is anything we can do to facilitate communication with our horse.

Communication
Hempfling suggests that in the course of growing up humans lose the "original body language", the "basic form of communication" and the "basic feel for movement and balance" that they once had as children. To learn to ride a horse – and hence, as a corollary to this,

to learn to interact with one at various levels – you, the human, need to "find your way back to what you once possessed". What you once possessed was a "basic form of archetypal communication". You also had a "natural self-assurance, self-determination and sense of self-preservation" which you need to rediscover and develop (p. 22).

The suggestion that Hempfling makes here is profound. Ask yourself what type of communication this could be, if there is no need for a child to learn it, because they possess it instinctively and indeed, if it is necessary for an adult human to experience a process of "unlearning many things", so that they can find their way back to what they once possessed (p. 22). Further on in this chapter Hempfling contends that (and the following quotation is printed in bold type in the book to underline its importance) **"above all, in order to gently but truly dominate a horse, it is absolutely necessary to communicate with him"**, and that horses have their own language, namely "body language" (p. 33). Is this what children have, according to Hempfling? Is this what adult humans need to rediscover? And if so, is this all?

The answer is not straightforward. While it is clear that children have not acquired the body language that is set out in detail in the book, they do possess its essence. The quotes mentioned above reveal that adults need to acquire both. So what is this essence? To find the answer to this question it helps to read the poem found on p. 45 of Hempfling's book, *The Horse Seeks Me*, which Hempfling follows with this conclusion:

> That is how the invisible shapes the visible, moves, renews and changes it. The body becomes the authentic and diverse instrument of the self-aware person; a sensitive way of expressing their individual personality. That is my understanding of body language.

The poem itself is about being in the moment without an agenda, a goal or any concerns. In other words, the essence of body language is being: consciously and authentically being yourself. Put another way, there is congruence between one's inner and outer self. You are not sending out conflicting signals as adults normally do. In her book, *Empowered Horses*, Imke Spilker sets this out so clearly, that it is worth repeating here:

> A person's inner "posture" and his external one create one unified image. Like the two sides of a coin they are inseparably connected to one another. Emotion reveals itself in movement. That is the problem with learned-by-rote body language manoeuvres as they are taught in clinics. If the gesture is not connected with genuine perception and feeling, it will generate incongruity and that will be perceived by an aware counterpart. "Beware of him whose belly does not move when he laughs," warns a Chinese adage. (p. 138)

Spilker then goes on to state the following:

> To be congruent, one with self, is a condition with which not many people are familiar anymore. Often we are not even aware of our disharmony, but its effect – particularly on horses – is very negative. At the same time we thoughtlessly demand this same sort of disharmony from our horses and try to force them into a similarly divided life. But a horse draws the majority of his power from the unbroken unity between expression and perception. In the language of a horse a particular gesture makes a particular statement. Moving in a certain manner is the direct expression of the experience of the moment. Every movement is a feeling! (p. 139)

Dominance and trust

Before exploring each of these concepts on their own, it is necessary to ask why Hempfling insists that both are required. He provides an answer in *Dancing with Horses* by noting that some of the vital characteristics of a dog and a cat can be found in every horse.

On the one hand, the horse is a herd animal in a way that is similar to the dog having their origins in a pack. A herd is a social group of horses within which there is a hierarchical order (which may be dynamic and changeable as opposed to static and constant). As such, every horse within a herd is either a follower or a leader in relation to every other member of that herd. Put another way, one is dominant, while the other is subordinate to it. Although horses may play with each and the stronger may allow the weaker to get away with conduct which would not be tolerated outside the bounds of play, when push comes to shove a dominant horse will always take the lead, while a subordinate one will follow it.

On the other hand, horses also exhibit the characteristics of a cat in their reliance on trust for benign social contact. Horses are also capable of deep friendships, even across species. Trust is an essential aspect of such a friendship but also of the relationship between a horse and the herd's lead stallion or mare. Yet you cannot win the trust of a cat by dominating it. Instead you need to be patient, gentle and tolerant.

This approach begs a seemingly irreconcilable question: how do you dominate a horse and simultaneously obtain its trust? Hempfling looks to the origins of European classical horsemanship for the answer as purportedly portrayed by the Christian knights. Their secret, he claims, is this:

> High-ranking horses have a quality which gives them the power to maintain their position without constantly having to fight for it. Once a person discovered this secret he would be able to dominate a horse without resorting to any form of physical force. He could caress and dote upon his horse a little in order to win his trust, as he would with a cat and, at the same time, he could dominate him with the same methods that the non-fighting lead stallion uses. This quite simply was and is the secret of the caballero, the knight. (p. 31)

Dominance

Hempfling insists that dominance is imperative, if a human is to set out on the path to the achievement of collected riding on a loose rein. He argues that it is essential for the psychic well-being of the horse that we dominate them completely, because it is only then that they will be able to achieve a peaceful state of mind and find their stability and equilibrium. This is even more important where a horse is engaged in fine, sensitive work, because "a horse who resists, even if only occasionally, can never be ridden with the finest, most subtle aids" (p. 29).

Definition of "dominance"

The terms, "dominance" and "domination", are frequently subject to emotive interpretations, which also seemingly vary from one person to the next. For this reason it is helpful to define these terms first. The free Oxford online dictionary (www.oxforddictionaries.com) defines "dominance" as "power and influence over others". In this context we may therefore define it as the power and influence which a human *has* over a horse. Used in this sense "dominance" therefore does not necessarily imply that the human actually dominates the horse – although this is not ruled out – and leaves room for an interpretation which sees the horse act of its own volition albeit under the power or influence of that human.

Definition of "domination"

The same dictionary defines "domination" as "the exercise of power or influence over someone or something, or the state of being so controlled".

Publicly opposed to any form of domination of horses while simultaneously successful in nurturing happy, self-collecting horses, Imke Spilker is perhaps the most appropriate person to define "domination" for us, even if she does not mention the term specifically when she does so. She defines it as "negative motivation":

> If we examine the current training of horses by people we find a classic example of negative motivation. The horse does something because he wants to avoid a negative consequence that the human being will inflict on him. The horse avoids something of which he is afraid or has learned to fear, and this "something" hangs in connection with an action of the human being. He runs so that he will not be attacked, so that the whip will not strike him, so that the spurs won't prick him. He stops so that his jaw will not be crushed, so that he will not be hit on the nose, or so that he will not again be chased round and round until he is totally exhausted. Horses try to avoid things that are unpleasant. Flinging out his forelegs so that no one whacks his sacrum, jumping high so that the pole does not hit those sensitive legs, running

because someone is sitting on his neck, faster, faster.... (p. 89)

She also defines it as "negative reinforcement":

> Traditionally, the stick reigns in the relationship between man and horse because a horse acts to avoid unpleasant consequences, not in order to get something for which it is worth striving. He reacts to the negative reinforcement. He is worked until he gives in, yields or moves forward. The horse learns about negative motivation and wants to avoid something worse. The reward is that the unpleasantness stops as the person lessens his actions (p. 90).

She also defines it as the use of commands, threats or punishment:

> We speak of an "aid" but we could just as well use the words, "command", "threat" or "punishment". Because logically structured systems are easier for human beings to deal with, riders learn this "aid-giving" as a set of rules, preferably with sketches that show them around the "dashboard" of this living sport machine. But to get a living being to function in such a predictable manner, a great deal of effort has to be invested to mechanise this creature and adapt him to the system. On this road to the goal of "animal automaton" occasional expressions of natural aliveness cannot be ruled out. When that occurs, disciplinary measures are used – sometimes harshly, sometimes more gently (p. 149).

She also defines it as the use of fear in the absence of force:

> Just because a horse is not physically touched by a person's movements does not mean that force is not being used. This is particularly the case in a confined space where the horse has no opportunity to retreat, as in a round pen, for example. After all, a situation does not become threatening only with the onset of physical contact. Threat arises long in advance of that, in the fear of the one being threatened "with the finger on the trigger". The person who pressures a horse against a wall or a fence or who drives him into a confined space is playing with the claustrophobia that is so much a part of the nature of these animals of the wide open spaces. Fear is, and will always be, the foundation of such work (p. 152).

Finally, she also defines it as having a horse do or refrain from doing something in the absence of its consent: "No matter what the particulars of the work, one thing always remains the same: horses are not asked for their consent" (p. 89). Indeed, whether a horse is asked for their consent or not marks the dividing line for Spilker between what type of training is acceptable and what type involves domination and is therefore not.

Interestingly, Spilker makes no mention of training by rote which is based on rewards only as opposed to the "carrot" and the 'stick' approach. Should one consider reward-based conditioned response training (such as clicker training) as something for which horses are asked to give their consent? Surely they have a choice where only rewards are involved? Obviously they do but the question that then needs to be considered is whether the conditioned responses that are elicited on demand do not constitute a form of domination by a human in that the horse ultimately does not consent to those responses (but only to the training preceding them) and that they are therefore not authentic movements on the part of the horse. Alternatively, one may conclude that no genuine communication is involved, as the conditioned responses only occur in response to a trigger.

Hempfling's dominance

Hempfling bases his dominance on a horse on what he refers to in *Dancing with Horses* (p. 32) as "two pillars", namely:

1. the qualities of a high-ranking horse, being magnetism, presence, dignity, superiority, thoughtfulness, experience and intelligence;
2. a system of signals with which a high-ranking horse is able to demonstrate and consolidate its power by the most peaceful means, and which are transmitted through body language.

Whether true or not, the knights embodied these qualities according to Hempfling. As he puts it:

> They knew exactly that they could only live and go to war with horses who gave them both absolute obedience and absolute

trust. They dominated their horses with the power of their personalities, their individual magnetism and with the help of those signals and gestures used exclusively by high-ranking horses in the wild. They cultivated the most humane interaction with their horses that you can imagine, because they took the place of everything, the entire herd, in their horses" lives. They gave their horses a solid dominance structure together with the opportunity for friendship.

All that is the foundation for collected riding on a loose rein. So we have to begin our work at the very beginning, at the time when the rift first developed between our body and our personality. (p. 32)

In the course of the seventeen years that separate the publication of the German version of *Dancing with Horses* and that of *The Horse Seeks Me*, Hempfling has remained committed to what he calls the "way of the knight" but he has changed his description of the two pillars and the change is profound. Dominance and trust have been replaced by "being and trust" (p. 61 – see also *Trust* below). Although there are occasional references to "dominance and trust" in the rest of the book (e.g. on p. 86, p. 118 and p. 315), the emphasis has shifted to the human becoming a caring, healing leader who is committed not only to not hurting the horse but to helping them grow and develop.

In *The Horse Seeks Me* Hempfling draws a distinction between the type of human who seeks to draw the horse down to the level of the unconscious human and the type of human who seeks authenticity and awareness in his interaction with horses. The first needs to seek the horse while the other allows the horse to find him, because he "is credible, sets an example, radiates inner confidence, is trustworthy, clear, unambiguous, relaxed, quiet, peaceful, positive, hopeful, balanced and controlled, and because he keeps on testing himself and, although he finds much that he does not like, he still remains cheerful and confident" (p. 39). This is the type of human we need to become, if we are to be capable of being with horses.

Hempfling's domination

Within Hempfling's approach the dominance of the human is so emphatic in the form of his presence that there is little or no need for him to actually dominate the horse. The questions of dominance and trust are resolved in the first few minutes and as of that time the horse, assured that the human will not in any way hurt him and is a trustworthy leader, does what is asked of them of their own volition not because they feel that they do not have any choice but because they want to do what is asked of them by the human whom they have acknowledged as their leader. Put another way, the absence of choice is irrelevant, because the horse does not want to consider any other option.

Punishment does not play a role in Hempfling's approach. As he puts it, "punishment as such has been purely and simply eliminated. This must always be the case...." (p. 198).

Nevertheless, Hempfling does insist on the human's need to protect his personal space. So what does Hempfling do if a horse ignores his signal to stop and intrudes into his personal space? "I hit him and very soundly!" (p. 199). What is important in this respect though, is that this is done reflexively and without anger, as a horse would do. What Hempfling also does is "immediately stroke the horse in the spot where I have just hit him" (p. 199). Can such self-defence be interpreted as domination? I personally feel that it can only be interpreted as self-preservation. Yet even if it could be interpreted as domination, the alternative – the injury or death of the human – is simply unacceptable. Hempfling also deals with this concept, which he now refers to as our "vital circle" on p. 213 of *The Horse Seeks Me* (p. 213).

Dancing with Horses contains numerous descriptions of what Hempfling refers to as dominance tools or aids. He cites backing-up as the most important dominance tool and suggests that it may be used in cases where your horse mouths you, rubs themself against you to scratch an itch or rub off a fly, or leave their position when being led:

> In all these cases and many others a few steps of backing up
> will send the horse back to his subordinate position. You
> always do this with a friendly demeanour and affection while
> emphasising your position. After three or four steps halt him
> and praise generously your now-obedient horse. (p. 199)

In *The Horse Seeks Me* Hempfling introduces another specific dominance tool, the "magic circle" (pp. 264-297). A description of the "magic circle" is provided on p. 271. Its stated purpose is not to dominate the horse but to improve the "dominance relationship" (p. 266).

The ostensible purpose of dominance tools is not to dominate the horse but to establish the human's dominance in the relationship between them thereby obviating the need for any dominating behaviour (i.e. domination). Although a dominance relationship does not necessarily imply the occurrence of domination as such, the existence of dominance tools presupposes the breakdown of such a relationship and the need to re-establish it. As such tools are not initially required to establish it and these tools do deprive the horse of any choice which they may have to refuse to cooperate, we may conclude that the re-establishment of a dominant relationship does involve domination, if we accept Spilker's broad definition of it as the denial of consent.

Going up a grade on Spilker's ladder of definitions, we may ask whether fear constitutes the foundation for the use of such dominance tools to re-establish a dominance relationship. It is clear that if these dominance tools are used as explained in *Dancing with Horses* and *The Horse Seeks Me*, no threat of violence is explicit or implied and, as such, there can be no room for fear to play a role.

Trust
Although Hempfling insists that trust is as important in a human's relationship with a horse as dominance, he devotes little attention to it in *Dancing with Horses*. Implicitly communication and dominance nurture it in that the former is intended to be clear but calm, while

the latter provides clarity and security. For the rest, Hempfling offers no help in relation to establishing trust let alone maintaining it.

It is to *The Horse Seeks Me* that we must turn for some direction as to how a human can establish and maintain trust with a horse. It is to be found in his comparison of the three ways of being with horses in the first part of Chapter 3. The human who follows the way of the knight (now based on "being and trust") is one who "works on his own unique qualities as a helper, mentor and healer, and on his exemplary leadership qualities, his body language and his coming to awareness, until the horse really wants to come to him, not because everything else has been spoiled for him and he simply gives up and gives in" (pp. 61-63). The implications are profound. The dominant position of the human is now defined by his capacity to give: to give help, guidance and healing to the horse. Such a person, Hempfling tells us, a horse wants to follow "because he believes and genuinely trusts in him". Such a person:

> becomes the central support for the free development of the horse. That is the fundamental principle. Everything revolves around the inner qualities of the person. In days gone by that was the (ideal and idealised) path of the knight. (p. 63)

Again though, Hempfling does not provide any guidance on how to obtain the horse's trust which is as detailed as when explaining how to achieve dominance over the horse. Add to this the fact that the horse appears to start trusting the human from the very moment that the human establishes their dominant position in relation to the horse, and we may have to conclude that it is not a question of the horse trusting the human but of them placing their trust in the latter. It is a fine point but an important one. We humans tend to trust someone based on experience. It is an active trust which develops and deepens over time. It is very seldom that we are prepared to place our trust in a stranger. If we do, it is usually based on the recommendation of someone whom we consider to be reliable, someone whom we trust: trust by proxy, as it were.

Horses, on the other hand, seem to place their trust in other horses almost immediately, albeit to varying degrees. A horse joining a new herd will almost immediately place its trust in the other horses comprising it and its lead horse (unless of course the new horse becomes the lead horse themself), submitting themself to the lead horse's dominant position. The horses comprising the herd graze and move together trusting each other that it is best for them to do so, and that it is safest for them to follow the lead horse. It is this act of placing trust which appears to occur when the horse submits to Hempfling's dominance, because it is a form of dominance that is accompanied by a commitment not only to refrain from hurting the horse but also to help them develop and grow. More importantly, we may conclude that the horse submits to the human subject to the latter's commitment to be trustworthy in this respect. This commitment and how it may be communicated to the horse is set out in detail on p. 121 of *The Horse Seeks Me*.

Conclusion

It is clear that we will need to experience considerable self-development if we are to become the credible human whom Hempfling insists we need to become in order to interact with horses, one who is capable of setting an example, who radiates inner confidence, is trustworthy, clear, unambiguous, relaxed, quiet, peaceful, positive, hopeful, balanced and controlled, and who keeps on testing himself and still remains cheerful and confident even though he finds much that he does not like. Fortunately, much of this self-development can occur through interaction with the horse.

Although such self-development will take a considerable period of time, there are some practical things we can start doing immediately. In *Dancing with Horses* Hempfling also provides the following exceedingly practical tips for improving communication with the horse (pp. 40-45):

1. everything is information – all that we do conveys information to our horse, which means that, unless we learn to use our body consciously, we may end up asking our horse to do something without being aware that we have done so, hence the need to learn to use our body properly;

2. less is more – the more aware we are of our body language, the calmer we will become and the less we will need to do in order to communicate with our horse, leading to an almost meditative type of interaction with it;
3. always use the same "vocabulary" – we need to be consistent in the body language that we use;
4. from flow to stimulus – if we ensure that our movements are controlled and flowing, only the smallest movement will be required to be detected by our horse as a stimulus to do or stop doing something;
5. softer, softer until you only think it – each signal needs to be increasingly refined, until the barest perceptible move will be enough to serve as an aid;
6. knock before entering – before asking our horse to do something, we need to alert them to the fact that we are about to ask.

Finally, we need to be aware that the horse communicates with us constantly and to learn to understand that communication. As Hempfling puts it:

> There are a number of very subtle signs and signals by which our equine partner lets us know if we are asking too much or too little. We must focus not just our eyes but our whole attention on these very subtle signals from our horses. If we do this, we will always have horses who approach their work joyfully, like children who play and, in playing, challenge and discover themselves.

Of these signs and signals there are two types which Hempfling cites in *The Horse Seeks Me* as indications that we are on the right path with our horse (p. 124). The first of these is what is translated in the book as the "first parallelism" (an unfortunate bit of gibberish) but should be more accurately referred to as the "first parallel", which occurs when the horse parallels what its human does (the horse moves forward, backward, to the left or to the right, or stops when his human does, doing so with "a natural consistency and at a slight distance" – see p. 79). "Another sign is complete peace, security, relaxation and contentment – they yawn with abandon" (p. 124). If either of these occurs, you know that you are on the right path. In short, be guided by your horse.

ON TOP OF THE MOUNTAIN: ACHIEVING A MAGICAL CONNECTION WITH YOUR HORSE

(The following book references are used in this article: IS – Imke Spilker, *Empowered Horses*, KFH – Klaus Ferdinand Hempfling, *The Horse Seeks Me* and MB – Michael Bevilacqua, *Beyond the Dream Horse*. See the Bibliography for more details.)

If you achieve this, if you recognise the horse and you have the chance to connect immediately, then something very important, very nice is occurring, because it is absolutely not important that the horse will gallop, that the horse will carry you, that the horse will one day do a shoulder-in or whatever kind of nice dressage figure, such as a piaffe or whatever is there, because you are realising there is no difference in perception. There is simply no difference in happiness. You are on top of the mountain.

From now on you can go from one top to another top to another top but it will not become better. The horse will not become happier. It's there from the first moment.

(Klaus Ferdinand Hempfling, Video: *Immediate Connecting with Horses, Part 2*, YouTube.com)

In the absence of a magical connection with a horse all that a human has to communicate with that horse is a technique, a method or a combination of techniques and methods. This may be enough to achieve some type of connection with that horse but that connection will not extend further than the technique employed and the horse will not give the human more than that technique elicits from it. This implies the existence of a major difference between a connection between horse and human that is merely based on a technique or method and one which is "magical". So what is that difference? To find out the answer to this question we need to learn what such a magical connection is, and to do this we may start by referring to those humans who have shown themselves to be capable of achieving such a connection with horses.

The magical connection

There are three humans whom I have turned to for guidance on what constitutes a magical connection with a horse and how to achieve it. They are Klaus Ferdinand Hempfling, Michael Bevilacqua and Imke Spilker. The reason why I have done so is because they are first of all committed to relating to horses without force or violence. Secondly, they put the horse first in the sense that the well-being of the horse represents the primary purpose of interaction between horses and humans. Thirdly, they rightly note that the key to doing anything meaningful with horses lies in developing a relationship with them and that any techniques and methods can only be secondary to this. And finally, their approach implies that if a human is to develop a relationship with a horse, that human will need to develop an authentic approach and presence.

So what, according to these people, is a magical connection between a horse and a human? Hempfling refers to the presence of "magic" (KFH, p. 167) which leads to what has become known as the "first parallel" (bizarrely translated as the "first parallelism" in his book – KFH, pp. 79-80). He describes the first parallel as follows:

> Basic trust is created after just a few moments. From there, horses follow me very precisely with a natural consistency and at a slight distance. They stand when I stand, and walk when I walk. (KFH, p. 79)

Referring to the first parallel as the "main focus of meditating with horse" (KFH, p. 80), Hempfling goes on to describe the experience as follows:

> Metaphorically speaking, it is as if there is a kind of "dip" in the ground beneath me and everything – including the horse – aspires to this "natural deepening". Scents, sounds, wind, sensations on the skin, cold, heat, the heaviness of my weight

on the ground, all of my limbs, my heartbeat, there is space for all of that in my perception and also for the whole appearance of the horse. There is nothing else. It is crucial that everything is very light, especially for the horse. (KFH, p. 81)

Here we have a description of profound presence along with the full internal and external awareness which it implies. So deep and all-embracing is it, that there is room for "nothing else". This then is one of the key aspects of the magical connection which Hempfling experiences in the first parallel. So important is the experience of the first parallel to Hempfling as the manifestation of the magical connection between horse and human, that he devotes several pages to various occasions on which he has experienced it. The first parallel is informed by authenticity – the human's ability to be genuine – and congruence – the human's ability to bring their external presence in line with their inner self – in every meeting with their horse. As Hempfling puts it:

Everything that I describe in this book concerning inner and outer presence and authenticity serves the first parallel. That is where everything comes together. Even if it happens when I first meet a horse, it is always a kind of recurring highlight for me. Each meeting with a horse should always be like a completely new one, and that is why the first parallel can happen again and again. (KFH, p. 83)

Imke Spilker also mentions something similar to the concept of parallel movement. She finds the magical connection with her horses through harmony and synchronicity at play. Horses and humans at play come to match each other intuitively while interacting with each other and this is exhibited in the course of the game:

It is reflected by all the participants – in their body carriage, in the rhythm of movement, in their identical reciprocal actions, and in a mutually agreed upon level of excitement, even including muscle tension, a total physical harmony. Play partners match one another. They find a common rhythm. They follow, respond to, and accompany one another. Instinctively, involuntarily, their rhythm, tempo, pace and momentum are synchronised and their movements are adapted to one another. (IS 74)

Although Michael Bevilacqua does not go into as much detail, he is conscious of a "connection stronger than any rope or bridle" (MB, p. 104).

Prerequisites for achieving a magical connection

Obviously a magical connection between horse and human cannot occur in a vacuum. Their interaction occurs within a specific framework and not just any horse and human are capable of achieving a magical connection with each other. Certain prerequisites need to be met by both horse and human as well as in relation to the framework within which their interaction occurs. These prerequisites are summarised below.

Horse

In the case of the horse these prerequisites are minimal and self-evident. The horse must be capable of:

- communicating with the human (see KFH on body language; IS 52);
- placing their trust in the human (KFH, p. 61; MB, p. 128; IS 82).

Human

All of our guides are clear that, if a human wishes to establish a magical connection with a horse, they will need to work on themself to satisfy an extensive array of requirements in terms of their self-development. Such a human must be capable of:

- experiencing spiritual and physical well-being (KFH, p. 35);
- being relaxed, peaceful, positive and hopeful (KFH, p. 39);
- being physically and spiritually self-aware, self-controlled, self-confident and simultaneously at ease (KFH, p. 39, 61, 121; MB, p. 77);
- being authentic and congruent (KFH, p. 8; MB, p. 42; IS 138);

- showing leadership (what Hempfling refers to as "dominance") and guidance in the interests of the horse (KFH, p. 61, 121; MB video; IS 81, 84);
- showing love, empathy, compassion and concern for the well-being of the horse and of reassuring it (KFH, p. 61, 63, 121; MB, p. 49, 99, 124, 129; IS 24, 50);
- being intuitive, sensitive, responsive and joyful, like a child (KFH, p. 30, 46, 79, 80, 225; MB, p. 42, 110, 151, 175; IS 24, 32, 6, 52);
- not expecting anything of the horse and of accepting that they may respond as they choose (KFH, p. 121, 217; MB, p. 49, 84, 124; IS 40, 53);
- intent or commitment in relation to all of the above (IS 45);
- communicating through body language and visualisation (KFH, p. 61; MB, p. 82; IS 28, 40);
- being fully present (KFH, p. 166);
- being trustworthy (KFH, p. 39).

This list is daunting in that it seems to suggest that the human will almost need to attain a state of perfection before they will be able to achieve a magical connection with a horse. While it is true that developing such a state of being would most certainly help a human to do so, it should be borne in mind that this list of qualities only applies in relation to horses and not fellow humans.

In addition, it should also be borne in mind that developing such a state of being is a process which occurs over a period of time. As this process unfolds, a human will be able to achieve a magical connection with horses with growing frequency and to maintain it for increasingly longer periods of time. Interaction with horses will also help a human develop such a state of being.

Interaction framework

The prerequisites applicable in relation to the framework for a genuine connection between horse and human are also fairly straightforward and self-evident:

- time must be made available for such interaction in the absence of a deadline (KFH, p. 86);
- such interaction must:
  - start on the ground (Hempfling's entire approach is premised on this; see also IS 41);
  - preferably occur in an enclosure which is safe and offers room for a horse to escape (hence, not in a round yard, which has an endless perimeter, the only escape from which is to move away from it and hence towards the human);
  - preferably occur in an enclosure which is not too big to render the initial meeting of human and horse impossible.

It should be noted that in Hempfling's case a magical connection is usually achieved in a highly controlled environment in the form of a small *picadero* (a square yard of about 11m by 11m).

Tips for achieving a magical connection
Naturally, the most important step you can take to ensure that you can consistently achieve and maintain a magical relationship with your horse is to embark on your own personal development to become the kind of human described above. Obviously, this represents a long-term solution which will not materialise overnight.

In the meantime though, there are many things that we can do immediately which will not only help us to achieve a magical connection with our horse with growing frequency but also to maintain it for increasingly longer stretches of time. When encountering a horse for the first time Hempfling generally recommends the following steps in the order in which they are mentioned (KFH, p. 74):
1. try and recognise the kind of horse in front of you;
2. try to gauge your horse's mood or frame of mind;
3. try to determine your next step on the path that you wish to take (this is done intuitively);

4. continue on this path with clarity and consistency while constantly communicating with the horse in a quiet and relaxed manner, understanding what is required.

Obviously, you will not need to perform Step 1 with your own horse, as you already know them. However, you may want to carry out Steps 2 to 4, although you may doubt whether you have attained the level of perfection achieved by Hempfling. His advice is that no one – not even your horse – is expecting perfection from you: "You just need to be heading in the general direction" (KFH, p. 74).

So how do you head in the general direction of perfection? Ultimately, only you and your horse can work this out together with the aid of the advice provided by our guides. Here are some of the tips which they provide to help us achieve the state of being required in a human who wishes to establish a magical connection with a horse, and which are working for me:

- make time available (KFH, p. 86);
- go into the moment, be entirely present and focus solely on the here and now (KFH, p. 46, 80, 166, 218; MB, p. 42);
- create distance and space between yourself and the horse until the latter relaxes and accepts your leadership (KFH, p. 222, 224, 226; IS 4, 36, 39, 49);
- try and sense the mood and personality of the horse (KFH, p. 79, 226);
- if you do not know what to do, do nothing until you intuitively do (KFH, p. 225, 226);
- ask instead of telling and avoid the boss mentality (KFH, p. 30, 39, 168; MB, p. 83, 161; IS 53);
- do not use any force or violence (KFH, p. 61, MB, p. 98, 142);
- be friendly, calm, patient, sensitive and responsive (KFH, p. 79, 227; MB, p. 16, 80, 93);
- do not try to establish a magical connection in the same way that you should not expect anything (the absence of expectation is central to Hempfling's teachings; see also MB, p. 49);

- accept what the horse does or refuses to do, as there is always a reason for it (MB, p. 84, 124; IS 40);
- deal with a refusal by either asking again creatively or accepting it for the moment (MB, p. 129);
- find joy in what you are doing and be ready to smile and laugh, even at yourself (KFH, p. 226; MB, p. 53).

Of the above tips avoiding the boss mentality has really been a challenge to me. When I get an idea and am ready to implement it, I tend to want to act on it straightaway. It has to happen and it has to happen now. The fact that there is a live animal objecting to this, is not an issue to which I am really keen on devoting a lot of time and energy. This used to be my approach and it is something that Hempfling also recognised in me. How I have tried to deal with it is described below.

My experience of a magical connection
The first real difficulty I experienced when trying to answer the question as to how I was ever going to learn how to achieve a magical connection with horses, was one that I myself created, inadvertently perhaps but no less effectively because of that. What I did was study all that Hempfling has written, watch all his videos, and speak at length with many who had attended his courses either as students or unpaid assistants. What I did not do was actually weigh up what it would really mean if I were to indeed do what he taught as conveyed through those channels, and then actually start acting on his teachings.

Ultimately, the guidance provided by other humans as to how to achieve a magical connection with a horse is merely that: guidance, and no more. It can help establish the framework, point you in the right direction and even dip your nose in it. At the end of it all, though, such guidance can do no more for you than you can do to get the proverbial horse to drink the water to which you have led them. In the same way that you cannot make the horse drink, so too such guidance is unable to get you to do anything. You have to do it yourself and you have to start now. The beginning of September, the time when I was supposed to be starting a year-long course of training with Hempfling, seemed to be an appropriate time to start doing just that. So I did and in the beginning there was nothing.

The decision that Vicki and I had then made to go on sabbatical for a year, meant that I had made the time available. This was an excellent start. My ability to go into the moment, which I have been working on with growing frequency every day since discovering body awareness exercises and Eckhart Tolle's *The Power of Now*, has also been indispensable. Having the time and being able to live it in the present have made it possible for me to surface from the almost suffocating hurt and anger that our experience with Hempfling produced and to discover a calm joy which I refuse to allow anyone to ever take from me again. This has created a context which is a *sine qua non* ("without which nothing") for achieving a magical connection with a horse: you are at peace, you have time, and you are *living now*.

It is within this context that I focused my conscious attempt to act on the above-mentioned tips in the course of September. As mentioned, in the beginning there was nothing. Anaïs would still insist on setting a blistering pace during our walks through the forest, break into a brief anxious trot now and then, and refuse to raise her head from grazing during our short breaks. The breakthrough came the day before we had a practice run to load Anaïs on to a trailer in preparation for her trip to the vet for her alternative treatment. Instead of halting or half-halting Anaïs when she threatened to get ahead of me, I consciously resolved to focus on leading through my presence. First, I started walking slightly faster than her until I was a little bit ahead of her. Then I focused my attention on my body, what I was feeling and where. Beyond that I became aware of the cool autumn air on my cheeks, a bird calling up to the right, the dank scent of the wet undergrowth, and then this massive warmblood striding hugely towards my left. There was just the two of us moving down the path in a cocoon of nature oblivious to everything else. Suddenly I sensed a slight hesitation in her stride and felt my body automatically respond to match her. She recovered and I joined her. That was when feeling turned to knowledge. I dropped my energy slightly and sensed her respond to match me. Then I raised my energy again and so did she. We went back and forth like this for several minutes before the contact slipped away as I caught my mind wandering again. What was left though, was the sensation of what had been: shared energy with half a ton of vibrant warmblood mare. Awesome, truly!

The next day we managed to establish this close contact again. Ineke, who owns the stables together with her husband, Kees, and who had made arrangements together with Jolanda for us to use a trailer for our trial loading run, came up to me in the morning and asked me how I planned to load Anaïs. I recall being rather nonplussed and slipping out an off-hand remark to the effect that it was simply a case of the mare following the leader whom she trusts. A few hours later I was called upon to be that leader. A small crowd of curious onlookers had gathered round, partly I suspect because we are those weird people who do not want to ride their horse before it can self-collect and who had intended to attend a year-long course with that Hempfling fellow in Denmark, and they wanted to see what it was that we would do differently when it came to loading a horse onto a trailer. I remember first showing Anaïs the trailer and treating it as though it was just another of the objects to be found in the courtyard in front of the stables. Then I walked her around the trailer and the courtyard in general while focusing on my body, Anaïs and the cocoon of our surroundings which we shared as we moved around. Everything else became a blur until Anaïs was in the trailer. Later Vicki mentioned that while I had been leading Anaïs towards the trailer, Daan, the teenage son of Ineke and Kees, had called out some advice to me, to which his mother had responded that I could not hear him even though I was only metres away from him. Indeed, I did not, because I was so present with Anaïs that nothing else mattered.

Interestingly enough, I could not load Anaïs onto the trailer a second time, because I was unable to achieve that connection again.

Since then I have found that I am able to establish a connection with Anaïs with growing frequency and that I am managing to maintain it for longer stretches at a time. The secret is not in knowing how to do it, because that is an activity of the mind. Rather, it is in feeling how to do it and knowing where to find that feeling. And the knowing refers to a knowledge of the tips provided by my guides, Hempfling, in particular. As he puts it:

> There is one thing I would like to mention, which is if somebody really wants to experience being in complete harmony with a horse, then I believe that in the end, they really have to *feel*. Until then, they will definitely keep on getting closer to this experience but they will not actually achieve it (KFH, p. 79 – emphasis added).

I do not fool myself that I am capable of replicating Hempfling and achieving complete harmony with a horse every time or that I can maintain it consistently while I am with a horse. That degree of presence and control I am still developing and will continue to do so with the help of Anaïs and any other horse with whom I may interact.

YIELDING TO PRESSURE: THE REALITY OF THE MYTH

Yielding to pressure, also known as pressure and release, the term refers to the core approach to training advocated by the conventional equestrian establishment, including the classical tradition, and yet it is also at the heart of the "natural horsemanship" movement which has evolved as a challenging response to the former. You will hear the term bandied about by instructors in horse training facilities around the world and trotted out tritely by their students, all intent on applying this approach when training horses to do what humans require of them. The approach it denotes has been the subject of numerous books and probably as many videos, if not more, while also constituting the core premise of most well-known training methods. Yet, when we strip away the jargon and rationale, how many of us fully realise what it entails and whether it is appropriate for training our equine friends, assuming that training itself is appropriate in a friendship, even if it is interspecies?

Yielding to pressure

When horse trainers refer to the application of the aids, they generally tend to mean the application of pressure to the horse followed by its release. The pressure is consistent and gradually increased until the horse yields to it by responding as the human intends, which is when the latter releases the pressure to reward – and hopefully (for the human applying the pressure) reinforce – that behaviour.

The internationally renowned Australian researcher and horse trainer, Andrew McLean, explains the process by setting it out in the following steps:

- only the targeted behaviour results in the release of pressure;
- the first pressure that the trainer applies is light because this will later transform into the signal;
- the pressure should be increased consistently. Any fluctuation constitutes a reduction in pressure and thus reinforces the wrong behaviour. Pressure is increased until the targeted response emerges;
- if intermittent pressures are used (nudging of the rider's legs or tapping of a long whip), there should be no pauses greater than one second so that the horse does not perceive the pause as reinforcing;
- at the onset of the targeted response the pressure should immediately be discontinued so that the horse recognises and associates the targeted behaviour with the reward.

(Andrew McLean, *The Truth about Horses*, pp. 41-42)

The theory is that at a certain point the horse's behaviour will become so reinforced and conditioned that only the lightest pressure (the "aid") will be required to elicit the targeted response. The result is that the horse's behaviour is modified to suit what the human requires of the creature, how the human requires it and when, namely, when the human applies the "trigger" of the aid.

Ultimately though, what this approach entails is the exposure of the horse to an experience which the human acknowledges is unpleasant to our equine friends but yet feels the need to do in order to train that sensitive creature.

The happy athlete

Around the world most humans who employ the pressure and release approach have the horse's well-being in mind in the course of training. At least, we should perhaps assume this to be the case based on the noble statements one may read in this respect in the rules or public relations materials published by the organisations representing or espousing the interests of those humans.

For instance, the FEI (International Equestrian Federation), which represents conventional equestrian pursuits states the following in Article 401 of its dressage rules:

The object of Dressage is the development of the Horse into a happy Athlete through harmonious education. As a result, it makes the Horse calm, supple, loose and flexible, but also confident, attentive and keen, thus achieving perfect understanding with the Athlete.

(Fédération Equestre Internationale (FEI) Dressage Rules, 25th edition effective 1 January 2014 including updates effective on 1 January 2015, p. 10)

Although the second sentence contradicts the first in that the latter refers to the horse as a potential happy athlete, while the former draws a distinction between the horse and the athlete (presumably, its human) with whom the horse is to achieve "perfect understanding", the sentiments are undoubtedly admirable. The horse's education is to be harmonious, a term which implies a form of education that is both commensurate with the horse's nature and conducive to the development of harmonious relations between horse and human. This implication would appear to be premised on the assumption that in the course of any training horse and human need to interact with each other as partners albeit while the latter assumes the leading role, as in a dance, and perhaps more importantly, that the well-being of the horse is as important as that of the human.

Questions

Yet, if the well-being of the horse is indeed as important in its interaction with us humans, perhaps we need to reconsider the pressure and release approach in the light of this. Perhaps we need to ask ourselves whether this approach is indeed compatible with the horse's well-being. And perhaps we need to do so in the light of the following concerns, which I have phrased in the form of questions:

- Are the aids indeed as light as what is generally claimed?
- As a form of negative reinforcement, is the pressure and release approach the most effective form of horse training and, more importantly, is it commensurate with our avowed commitment to the well-being of our equestrian friends?

- More profoundly, is the pressure and release approach actually compatible with the nature of the horse?
- Is it not indicative of an attempt to dominate and control horses instead of empathising and empowering them?
- And if it is, is this approach not exploitative even if the horse does not object to it?
- Moreover, does the pressure and release approach not objectify the horse and reduce this sensitive animal to the status of an accessory to a human's pursuits?
- As importantly, is the pressure and release approach not dehumanising in that it is a mechanistic one relying predominantly on the use of mechanical aids in the absence of any true human presence and input?

"Lightness"

It is a term that holds appeal. "Lightness": it conjures up images of graceful movement, almost ethereal in the near-levitation which it implies. It is with lightness that we must ride and apply the aids.

And just what exactly are those aids that we must lightly apply? Pressure and release or yielding to pressure, of course, but is that all? Do we not do this with the aid of tools which have the capacity to injure and maim? The saddle through which we communicate direction, movement and rest, does it not begin to compromise the tissue in the horse's back within about fifteen minutes, especially the western variant, which is usually heavier and larger? What of the spurs? Do they not dig into flesh which is sensitive enough to detect a fly alighting on it? And at the apex of refined riding, dressage, do we not employ a curb bit with leverage massive enough to break the jaw in which it rests, frequently in combination with a snaffle bit, the use of either or both of which frequently require the modification of the horse's physique in the form of the removal of a tooth? Even the more refined versions of riding, whether they are dubbed classical equitation, straightness training, centred riding or some other ostensibly enlightened term, do they also not demand the use of a massively leveraged bit?

Of course, there are many humans who rationalise the use of such instruments of force. They argue that the horse does not object to them. Some even contend that the horse seeks to be privy to them in order to acquaint themselves with our world. Perhaps they are right. Possibly, they may have misinterpreted the horse's forward-pointing ears to mean much more than that they simply know no better. But let us be generous and assume that the horse actually enjoys the application of such instruments of force, perhaps a little like a member of a sect who offers her soul and her body to its leader's whims of self-gratification and indulgence, firm in the conviction that this will lead to her salvation. Even then we might ask whether the victim's acquiescence, surrender to or even embrace of her exploiter's abuse excuses the latter of his responsibility to respect the personal integrity of his victim. So too, should we not ask whether the horse's complicity in its subjugation excuses us from our duty of care to safeguard their well-being?

Yet let us be even more generous and assume that these instruments of force are used so lightly – at least by those experts who are capable of employing highly leveraged instruments of force without resorting to such leverage – that the horse is not forced to do or refrain from doing anything. Even then could we not legitimately ask whether the horse is not acting under duress, its behaviour compelled by the threat of force, especially in the light of the training that is the inevitable precursor of such "lightness"?

Negative reinforcement

Andrew McLean is probably not alone in arguing that the pressure and release approach represents the most effective form of training precisely because it constitutes a form of negative reinforcement, that is, a method which involves the application of an increasingly unpleasant experience until the horse produces the desired behaviour. At that point the horse is "rewarded" with the termination of that unpleasant experience in the form of the removal of the pressure involved.

Although the reasoning is eminently logical, perhaps we humans may want to consider the nature of the application of pressure. I know of no scientific study of the pressure and release approach to horse training which not only does not acknowledge that the application of pressure constitutes an unpleasant experience to the horse but also does not recognise that its unpleasant nature represents the very basis for its efficacy. As such, we may wish to ask ourselves whether we are really acting in the best interests of the horse by subjecting it to such an unpleasant experience. Would you really want to do this to a creature whom you claim to love?

Then again, perhaps it is possible to present a legitimate argument to the effect that it is entirely acceptable to subject a horse to an unpleasant experience on a regular basis for the purposes of eliciting behaviour from them which is entirely in the interests of their well-being. For instance, this could be argued in the case of straightness training, which is designed to teach the horse to carry themself straight, although one might question whether this does not serve any purpose other than to carry a human while simultaneously mitigating the risk of personal injury due to that very act, one for which the horse was not designed.

Again let us be generous and assume that it is possible to present a legitimate argument to this effect. Even then we may wish to question the rationale for adopting such an approach, if only because available evidence reveals the relative inadequacy of negative reinforcement as a method of horse training. In recent years a growing body of evidence has come to show that the pressure and release approach is significantly inferior to positive reinforcement methods of horse behaviour modification (such as clicker training) in terms of both the speed at which behaviour is modified and the relative permanence of such modification, as well as the obvious benefits it yields in the form of a positive attitude on the part of the horse. In that it also involves the reward of desirable behaviour in the absence of the application of an undesirable experience, a rapidly growing number of humans are also embracing positive reinforcement as a preferred approach to horse training.

Nature of the horse
Perhaps the most profound reason for questioning the use of the pressure and release approach to training lies in the fact that it fails to take the nature of the horse into account. It fails to do so in that it:

1. does not acknowledge that horses may react differently to the same type of pressure depending on the nature of the horse concerned and the circumstances in which it finds itself;
2. ignores the fact that horses react differently to different types of pressure.

A closer examination of each of these points may reveal that the pressure and release approach to training fails to accommodate the nature of the horse to a significant extent.

1. Horses react differently to pressure
Here we can draw a distinction between the individual responses of different horses, on the one hand, and the different responses exhibited by one and the same horse in different situations.

a) Individual responses of different horses
Horses are individuals and, as such, respond differently to pressure. This statement may be trite but it is very true and I do not have to leave my domain to ascertain that this is the case. For instance, the difference in the response of our two mares, Pip and Anaïs, to any physical pressure which they perceive to be threatening is that of day and night. Whereas Pip will initially resist but eventually yield if the perceived threat appears to be overwhelming, Anaïs is inclined to resist with growing intensity until she is transformed into a potentially dangerous monster.

b) Different responses by the same horse
Have you ever noticed that the same horse can respond differently to pressure from one situation to another? Let us take slapping as an example, and here I am referring to a pretty hard slap anywhere on

the horse's body with the exception of the head and between the hind legs. What would normally happen if you were to slap your horse nice and hard? They would move away, would they not? Of course they would.

What? You do not slap your horse? Never? What if I were to tell you that I do and not just my horse but my wife's too? What if I were to tell you that my wife slaps her mare and mine too? And what if I were to tell you that both our horses come to us when they want to be slapped and position their bodies in front of us, so that we can deliver the slap to exactly where they require it? Actually, our horses do not normally do this. They only do so in the summer when swarms of horse flies descend upon them from the nearby forest and corn fields, reducing their lives to fly-bitten misery. Even when wearing fly mesh, there are still occasions when a horsefly alights on the mares' thin summer coats and the only sure way of liquidating it is to slap it smartly. Our horses know that we are helping them when we do this and they are willing to accept the slaps – and even beg for them – if this is what it takes to eliminate the pests.

2. Horses react differently to different types of pressure
One does not have to venture far into the practice of equine training before encountering the "generally accepted" notion that a horse ultimately responds in the same way to any form of pressure, irrespective of whether that pressure is accompanied by physical contact or not. Taken to the extreme, there are some who even claim that the mere entrance of a human trainer into the presence of a horse is enough to apply pressure to that creature and that the horse will respond in the same way all along the scale from that "pressure" to that of a spur dug viciously into the animal's side. Indeed, so prevalent is the assumption that a horse responds the same way to all types of pressure, that it is tempting to conclude that this notion is almost universally elevated to the ethereal heights of equine training dogma. There are relatively few humans who seem prepared to challenge this fundamental principle imposed on equine training, yet

every horse initially does so until ultimately compelled to act accordingly.

Yet if we were to allow a horse to express themself in response to the full range of such different types of pressure and to take the time to observe their response, we would see a variety of natural responses from one and the same horse. And that variety would depend on the type of pressure applied. But before examining the various types, it is perhaps useful to define what we mean by "pressure". The online Oxford English dictionary has the following two definitions of pressure:

1. continuous physical force exerted on or against an object by something in contact with it;
2. the use of persuasion or intimidation to make someone do something.

(https://en.oxforddictionaries.com/definition/pressure – consulted on 13 August 2017)

The first definition refers to pressure accompanied by physical contact, while the second is not. This distinction is also useful for the purposes of examining how a horse normally responds to such different types of pressure.

a) Pressure with physical contact

So how does the horse challenge the human dogma of yielding to pressure? In the first place, it is in the nature of most horses to draw a clear distinction between pressure accompanied by physical contact exerting that pressure, pressure accompanied by physical contact not exerting that pressure, and "pressure" that is not accompanied by physical contact.

Where pressure is applied and is accompanied by physical contact exerting that pressure, horses tend to do the very opposite of yielding to such pressure, at least initially before training has advanced far enough to successfully demand the requisite response of yielding, although it should be borne in mind that the horse's response will then be a conditioned one and not how they would respond of their own volition in the absence of such training. The untrained natural response of most horses to physical pressure is not to yield to it but to resist it and to do so with increasing force until that pressure is strong enough to overcome the horse's resistance. The reason for this is probably twofold. When such physical pressure is initially applied, the horse's muscles automatically resist it. The horse is physiologically primed to respond in this way. As such, it is not a cognitively ordered process. If this response fails to secure the release of that physical pressure, which it is designed to do, many if not most horses would then be likely to enter panic mode and resist it even more fiercely, prompted largely by their instinctive propensity to flee perceived danger, a factor which plays such a prominent role in their response to pressure in the absence of physical contact, which is dealt with below.

Then there is pressure that is accompanied by physical contact which does not physically exert that pressure. This type of pressure I discovered entirely by chance while trying to ask a horse in my care to raise their head from their pile of hay to allow me to clean their eyes (I preform a good deal of physical care while the horses eat, as they seem to be much calmer and more amenable). Describing how I do this may perhaps illustrate what I mean more graphically than an abstract attempt at explanation. Essentially, I place my hand under the jaw of the horse while standing just in front of their shoulder almost underneath their neck. Fully present in the moment, I suddenly stand up erect, all my energy and intent directed at ensuring that the horse raise their head but my hand below their jaw, while remaining present, does not itself exert any physical pressure and merely serves as a conduit for the energy. This action I might accompany with a verbal request, such as "Head up". Although I do not usually need to employ this technique as the horses habituate themselves quite quickly to routines, it does illustrate horses' sensitivity to energy and the resultant difference in their response to the physical exertion of pressure.

b) Pressure without physical contact

Where pressure is not accompanied by physical contact, horses tend to respond differently on the whole. Instead of resisting such pressure, they appear to be more inclined to yield to it and to do so far more readily than in the case of physical contact. In this case too the reason is quite straightforward in that it lies within the nature of horses to do so. All too frequently we humans trot out the trite mantra to the effect the horses are creatures of flight. When faced with a perceived danger, they almost instinctively seek to flee first. Well this is precisely what explains in part why they are likely to yield to pressure in the absence of physical contact, especially if it is perceived to be an actual or potential threat. The other part of the explanation may largely be found in the nature of the horse as a sentient being devoid of the baggage of rational thought. To a horse, life is a constant, experiential affair experienced through their senses and the energy they feel. In the absence of physical contact, pressure assumes the form of energy and how horses sense and feel about it, which is to say, how they experience it.

Viewed from an external perspective, horses appear to respond very differently to contact-free pressure, depending on whether they perceive such pressure to be focused on them or not. Indeed, it is precisely this distinction which is so clearly discernible in herd behaviour. By way of an example, in one of the herds in which my mare, Pip, spent part of her life there were two geldings, a heavily built Dutch warmblood called Bentley and a grey Polish quarter horse dubbed Duke. At the top of the pecking order, Bentley could pass calmly through the herd without causing any consternation and any horse in his path would defer to him and move out of the way with a similar degree of calm. All the other horses acknowledged his status as the dominant presence in the herd and yielded to that presence in the knowledge that any pressure which they may have experienced was not directed against them.

Duke, on the other hand, was an aggressive, maladjusted individual who felt a constant need to charge any horse that he felt was entering his rightful domain or was close enough to do so. As a result all of the other horses with exception of the acknowledged leader, Bentley, were frequently sent scattering, almost always creating potentially dangerous situations. Duke directed his aggression towards his herd mates and they responded by ducking out of the way and rushing off to escape his perceived reach. Instead of simply moving out of his path, as they did with Bentley, safe in the knowledge that no aggression was being directed towards them, they immediately felt Duke's focus on them and responded accordingly.

It is precisely this difference in focus, this indirect pressure (the pressure being on the path, as it were, and not on any horse obstructing it) which Klaus Ferdinand Hempfling exploits so effectively in his work with horses. By assuming the energetic presence of a creature at the peak of the pecking order, one who does not entertain any doubts about that presence and who therefore has no need to resort to dominant behaviour, Hempfling indirectly induces a horse to acknowledge his presence, respect it and ultimately follow it. Those humans, on the other hand, who fail to acknowledge this important difference in focus are left with little choice but to adopt the presence of a Duke, securing compliance through the threat of force. And like Duke, the source of such aggressive behaviour ultimately lies in impotence. Powerless in the absence of any meaningful alternative, the human resorts to unsocial behaviour towards one of the most sociable creatures on the planet.

I find this indirect pressure particularly useful when distributing hay in a small herd of horses. Holding my hand higher than and in front of my head to create the illusion of a "bigger me" with the hay held in my other arm away from the horses, I move determinedly through the herd without looking at any horse directly and they generally back or turn out of the way, although on occasion I may need to motion them away with a slight but "intentful" (full of intent – a word waiting to be invented) wave of my erect hand.

There is another form of pressure in the absence of physical contact which horses respond to without feeling threatened. I call it oblique pressure, as it is a combination of aspects of direct and indirect pressure. In this case the pressure is directed at the horse but without facing the animal or looking them in the eye. Although the horse is aware that they are being challenged, they do not experience this type of pressure as threatening, because it does not appear to be directed at them personally, as it were. I find this type of pressure particularly useful for asking a horse to reconsider their decision to abandon their pile of hay to chase a fellow species member away from theirs because they perceive it to be bigger or better. In this case I position myself between the dominant horse (as in higher up the pecking order) and the subordinate animal (as in lower down the pecking order) and respond to every step of theirs with one of my own blocking access to the other pile of hay. Calmly and patiently we conduct our little dance, until the message sinks in and the dominant horse returns to their own pile of hay.

Domination and control

To the extent that the application of pressure is designed to secure the horse's compliance without affording them the opportunity to decline, it amounts to a form of domination and control on the part of the human responsible for it. This is because such pressure is designed to force or compel a horse to do or refrain from doing something as that human requires. This also applies where such pressure and its accompanying intent are manifested in the lightest form possible, because in this case there is always the underlying threat of the pressure being applied more forcefully.

In this respect the FEI must be commended in being so disarmingly honest in its dressage rules. Let us return to the FEI's statement of the object of dressage, namely, the "development of the Horse into a happy Athlete through harmonious education," which "makes the Horse calm, supple, loose and flexible, but also confident, attentive and keen, thus achieving perfect understanding with the Athlete". This statement is immediately followed by the assertion that:

These qualities are demonstrated by:
- the freedom and regularity of the paces;
- the harmony, lightness and ease of the movements;
- the lightness of the forehand and the engagement of the hindquarters, originating from a lively impulsion;

- the acceptance of the bit, with submissiveness / "throughness" (*Durchlässigkeit*) without any tension or resistance.

Here we have it from the horse's mouth as it were. The insistence not merely on domination and control but, more importantly, on the horse's submissiveness is stated with refreshing candour. The horse is required to accept the bit (two are actually used simultaneously at the peak level of FEI dressage) and be submissive in the absence of any tension or resistance. Anyone who seriously pursues dressage in line with FEI dressage rules is unambiguously required to dominate and control their horse by compelling it to be utterly submissive. Indeed, the stipulation to the effect that such submissiveness should not be accompanied by any tension or resistance would to all intents and purposes suggest that learned helplessness is required on the part of the horse.

Objectification of the horse
As such, the horse is reduced to playing the role of a cog – albeit an important one – in a machine which its human has devised to achieve a goal defined by that human, no matter how noble and laudable it may be. Because the horse is denied a choice, they are stripped of their individuality and become a mere object in service to the human's grand design and, as such, are ultimately little more than an accessory to the human's ego and/or pursuit of self-enrichment. Usually, this also occurs at the horse's expense in that this occurs to their physical, psychological and/or emotional detriment.

Self-justifying fallacy
Yet how many of us humans will be able to resist the temptation to object to this critique of the pressure and release approach by pointing out that the horse's ears are forward, their eye is bright and they are "forward". Clearly, the horse must be enjoying what they are doing, even if they are doing so by yielding to pressure.

This is an argument that exhibits a logic which is similar in its self-justificatory nature as that of the assertion that the leader of a sect is not exploiting his (they are usually male) followers (they are predominantly female) by taking their money and/or using their bodies, because what is taken has been freely given. The assumption is that only the victim of such exploitation is responsible for it and that the perpetrator is exempt from bearing any responsibility for it by virtue of the victim's willing submission.

I have yet to understand why anyone who knowingly exploits another creature should not bear responsibility for such exploitation irrespective of whether or not the victim knowingly and wittingly submits to it, where that victim is an adult human. How much more responsible is such a perpetrator where the victim is a creature that is entirely dependent on them and is unable to make the choices which an adult human, in full control of their mental faculties and acting entirely rationally and reasonably, is capable of making?

Consequently, does the assertion to the effect that the horse consents to and even enjoys the application of the pressure and release model not only amount to the abdication of such responsibility on the part of the human applying it but also the amoral employment of that assertion to justify their actions. In that the assertion lacks veracity, is it not fallacious? And in that it also seeks to justify the perpetrator's actions, is it not a self-justifying fallacy?

Self-perpetuating fallacy

Perhaps the most insidious aspect of the myth of the yielding to pressure approach lies not so much in the false assumptions on which it is premised, as discussed above, but in the temptation it holds for humans to justify the constant application of that approach. This is at once most decisively and most deceptively evident in the starting point which asserts that all interaction with a horse inevitably involves the exertion of pressure on it by a human with some commentators even contending that such pressure is readily evident in a horse's immediate response to a human entering its presence, which is one of alarm.

This approach is deceptive in that it is invariably postulated as an unquestionable, self-evident universal truth, whereas it is most decidedly not. In the first place, what is frequently taken to be a horse's recognition of pressure when a human enters its presence is little more than an acknowledgement of what comes entirely naturally to the species known as *equus caballus* and is an intrinsic part of its physiological makeup: a finely honed sensitivity to energy and in this case that of the human who seeks to interact with it. Secondly, evidence militating against this assumption may also be found in the fact that horses sometimes ignore a human who enters their presence. Indeed, it is often this refusal on the part of the horse to acknowledge that a human has anything remotely interesting to contribute through their presence which serves as the basis for the adoption of the pressure and release approach. After all, what other course of action is left to a human whose horse so mercilessly exposes their impotence? Actually, there is another course of action open to the human but it is bound to make such demands on their character that they almost always opt for the seemingly more effective approach of pressure and release for no other reason than that it is easier on them and appears to secure almost immediate results.

Similarly, this approach is decisive in that it serves as its own rationale for its adoption and application. The logic involved goes something like this: because a horse always feels pressure exerted on it by any human who chooses to interact with it, the human has no option but to employ that pressure in such interaction. As such, the only question that remains is how that pressure should be applied and how much should be involved.

In that this approach is based on false assumptions, as explained above, is it not fallacious? In that it also serves as its own rationale, is it not a self-perpetuating fallacy? And in that an approach such as this, which is so hostile to the horse, masquerades as a logical, reasonable one, is it not also insidious?

Non-enlightened

To the extent that the pressure and release model exhibits all of the flaws discussed above, is it not a non-enlightened method that is diametrically opposed to an empathetic, empowering approach which is designed to encourage the horse to become a willing partner in the dance with the human?

A choice

It is important to realise that a human has a choice in how they interact with a horse. Far from being unavoidable, requiring our equine friend to yield to any pressure we exert represents a choice that we make in relation to such interaction. There are other ways of interacting with a horse, although they may make demands on us which may initially seem to be incomprehensible initially and, once understood, daunting. Should this deter us? Perhaps the answer depends on what type of relationship we seek with our horse.

The alternatives?

So what alternatives are available? One alternative which almost immediately suggests itself is positive reinforcement, especially as exhibited through clicker training. What are the benefits? Are there any disadvantages? Here are some other ideas which we might also wish to consider in the course of any discussion of possible alternatives:
1. tapping into the horse's sensitivity as an energetic being;
2. tapping into the horse's capacity for play;
3. tapping into the horse's capacity for friendship;
4. tapping into the horse's desire to follow a reliable, trustworthy creature;
5. becoming the kind of human a horse seeks to be with.

Impotence of the human

Klaus Ferdinand Hempfling contends that, if we are to truly become the kind of human a horse seeks to be with, we will need to develop our physical and spiritual potential to the extent that horses recognise in us someone who is completely and authentically present with them in the here and now, someone whom they can trust in that we are dependable and decisive, and someone who is able to communicate with them using their mother tongue, feeling and body language. To the extent that we are incapable of doing this, we find it necessary to rely on an external approach employing external aids: pressure and release coupled with all the implements of compulsion and restraint that are essential to such an approach.

As such, to the extent that we rely on it, the pressure and release approach reflects the impotence of the human who resorts to it, namely, our inability to be the kind of human a horse seeks to be with. Indeed, in this respect we might wish to postulate a theorem to the effect that the more a human endeavours to apply physical pressure in their interaction with the horse or to threaten to do so, the more tools they require to apply that pressure or threaten to do so, the more force they need to bring to bear when applying such pressure or the more severe the threat they imply when wielding the means to do so, the greater the impotence they exhibit in their dealings with their horse. As such, until we abandon the pressure and release approach in our interaction with horses, will we humans not always be confessing our impotence in our dealings with those sensitive creatures? And if we will, how much longer do we wish to continue to do so?

HORSE TRAINING: LIVING THE DREAM OR CREATING AN ILLUSION?

If you have a horse, you train the creature surely? And if you cannot train your horse yourself, you get someone in to do the job for you, don't you? After all, is not the horse like a computer in that, if there are any bugs in the system which prevent them from performing as required, you simply upgrade the operating system, in this case through training? And surely your horse will then be able to do what you want it to once the new operating system has been installed? A former student of Klaus Ferdinand Hempfling and now a "horse trainer" in her own right once taught me that this was possible, using a similar software metaphor. Perhaps it is true, for training can indeed allow you to "drive" your horse like a car in response to your use of the equine equivalents of steering wheel, gears, brakes and accelerator. But when your equine friend is prancing around the ring strutting their stuff in response to your aids and cues, will there be anything left of the spontaneous, proud, sensitive, supremely conscious being that a horse has the potential to be or become? And will you and your horse be living your equestrian dream? Or will you simply have created nothing more than an utter illusion?

Purpose of horse training

So what is the purpose of training a horse? It goes without saying that the answers to this question may be as varied as the types of training that are practised and the views of their practitioners, proponents and critics, with those answers being as specific as the type of training involved. For this reason alone it is advisable to confine ourselves to a more general view of training and pose the question as a two-pronged one. Firstly, why do humans generally decide to train horses? And secondly, what do they hope to achieve by doing so? Because these two prongs are so closely related to each other, they are dealt with here as two sides of the same coin.

In general, humans train horses for one or more of the following main reasons (this list not being exhaustive):

- utilitarian in the sense that the horse is required to perform a specific job for the benefit of the human community, the training given to the horses used by the mounted police serving as a good example of this;
- financial gain, which may vary from subsistence on the part of poverty-stricken individuals to the enrichment of an already comfortable if not wealthy elite, the former's use of the horse being perhaps understandable, the latter's probably questionable;
- social standing, where one's social rank or status is partly determined by the ability to control a horse;
- sport, which involves the horse serving as the primary means and accessory to a human's sporting achievements, even though it is the horse that is chiefly responsible for those achievements;
- leisure, which entails that the horse is there to serve solely as a means of conveyance for the pleasure of the human whom it is required to carry;
- human therapy to the extent that the horse is used to help humans cope with or overcome physical or mental limitations;
- human training to help humans develop "emotional intelligence" and interact more closely with each other (in many cases for the pursuit of financial gain);
- therapeutic in that it is designed to help the horse learn to carry themself straight and in a balanced fashion, more frequently than not to ensure that they are capable of carrying a human while minimising the physical harm which this activity can cause;
- the pursuit of a dream to connect and dance with what is arguably the animal species that has not only captured the imagination of humans more emphatically than any other throughout their history but has also exerted more influence on human development than any other. Here "dance" is used as a metaphor denoting any form of mutually beneficial interaction

involving willing horse and human partners which may give rise to an expression of creativity and beauty that is greater than that of which each partner is capable of producing on their own. This is the "dream".

The dream

It is the pursuit of this dream that is the primary focus of this discussion of horse training, for the other main reasons why humans seek to train horses entail an approach which is largely mechanistic and attainable to some or other degree. They are mechanistic to the extent that they can be achieved through the application of techniques designed to do just that. And they are attainable to the extent that the employment of such techniques facilitates that. Put another way, all humans can make a horse do something and merely differ in how we do this, whereas the real test is whether we can find it within ourselves to become the kind of human with whom a horse chooses to be a willing partner.

This is where the dream comes in and it is elusive. And it is so not only because it eludes our every effort to capture it but especially in that the more we try to do so, the more likely we are to fail. And yet, paradoxically, when an example of such "capture" is presented to us, we try even harder to replicate it, sparing neither money nor effort to do so.

There is a video on YouTube which depicts the dream so vividly and emphatically that it has been viewed far more often than any other of its type (a little under 2.9 million times by mid-August 2017). It features Klaus Ferdinand Hempfling interacting with Ferdinand, a classically trained Lipizzaner stallion, out in an open field without any restraints or other hardware on the horse. Using a coiled rope held aloft at the shoulder to ask for collection and a long whip extended towards the inside hock to prompt the extension of the hind-leg forward and underneath the belly, Hempfling helps the stallion find his balance while collecting himself and flexing laterally. This is clearly the result of intensive training. Nevertheless, when unfettered in the open field the horse is at liberty to run off at any time and does so, only to return again and resume his interaction with the man. Interspersed between segments of trained interaction, there are moments of spontaneous play and calm closeness. The clip ends with horse and human slowly walking back home together. You can view the video here: https://www.youtube.com/watch?v=-zq06bmJLt-U (without the hyphen – I recommend turning off annotations in the settings menu, as well as the sound).

This video has probably been more instrumental in securing clients and a following for Hempfling from around the world than any other single tool which he has in his marketing toolbox. And the reason for this lies in the power of the dream which it depicts. Although training was responsible for much of the interaction depicted, it is clear that horse and human share a deep connection with each other which extends into their shared moments of spontaneity. The horse is alert, alive and powerful but soft, while the human is calm but so reassuringly present to the point of being the anchor to which the stallion is drawn. The connection between horse and human is magical. It is the essence of the dream.

The training carrot

Thousands of humans have gone to Hempfling for guidance over the years and many thousands more have sought a little of that same guidance in his books, articles, documentaries and video clips, yet very few seem to have understood the path that he has shown them or, if they have, may have found it impossibly hard to summon the self-discipline required to pursue it. For Hempfling is a man who has himself sought guidance in the physical and spiritual symbiosis underlying ancient Chinese traditions, the *I Ching* and martial arts (especially elements of Tai Chi) which those traditions spawned, in particular. From these and other sources he has developed his own approach to body and spiritual awareness which repackages the essence of those traditions with a distinctly European flavour drawing inspiration from romanticised views of Celtic society and the Knights Templar.

Although Hempfling is known as a horseman and has been viewed at times as a practitioner of natural horsemanship, he draws a sharp distinction between his way, on the one hand, and on the other, natural horsemanship and conventional equestrian approaches, criticising both and postulating his as the way forward, at least for himself and, by implication, anyone wishing to be guided by him. The essence of this approach (at least in the form in which it is communicated) lies in an acknowledgement, however implicit, that any meaningful interaction between a human and a horse is only possible if there is a true connection between them, one which sees the horse willingly choose to be with and be guided by the human. The existence of such a connection presupposes a level of communication between the species which will enable them to ask and respond to each other. This in turn presupposes the existence of contact between horse and human. Put another way, the horse needs to acknowledge the presence of the human as emphatically as the human does the horse. Yet how can the human achieve this without force or the threat of it?

To Hempfling the answer lies in the human and not the horse. It is the human who needs to undergo physical and spiritual development if they are not only to learn how to fully enter the dimension in which the horse lives – the here and now, that is, always in the moment – without any emotional or other baggage but also to become the kind of human whose presence a horse acknowledges and also chooses to follow, as it were. In short, the human needs to start, not with the horse, but with themself. This spiritual development is not some "pie in the sky" but a down-to-earth pursuit of conscious living and movement. As an aid towards the achievement of this Hempfling has developed special body awareness exercises, essentially a form of meditation in motion which enables physical and spiritual consciousness to merge within the human in the form of a strong but empowering presence.

As someone who is inspired by and has to some extent experienced this approach, I can vouch for the fact that it is highly effective. Although I will most probably never be a master who is capable of dancing with horses in public, I am humbled by the fact that our horses place their trust in us to such an extent that I have no need for force or the threat of force when I am consciously interacting with them in the moment. (This is not to deny that the temptation to play the boss with my horse does not surface at odd times and far too frequently for my liking). Getting to this point, however, is not easy. It requires constant self-discipline and awareness, if you want to get it right all of the time.

And herein lies the rub. Most humans in search of a more horse-friendly approach seem to be intent on confining their search to more benign ways of controlling their horse rather than themself. They are willing to explore all avenues, self-proclaimed trainers, methods, techniques and tools that appear to be designed to do just this to the extent that their budget allows. Some are even prepared to attend more than one of the most expensive courses available, those provided by Hempfling himself, but they are reluctant, if not downright unwilling, to exercise the self-discipline and self-development which he preaches. Training becomes the new carrot to the human, not of themself, but of the horse. This raises the question as to whether horse training is an effective and appropriate substitute for the self-development of the human in pursuit of the attainment of the dream described above. In order to answer this question we need to understand what training involves and entails.

Training theory

There are many humans who are far more familiar with conventional training theory than I am and who are more capable of explaining it to you. In the course of such an explanation you are likely to hear terms bandied about, such as "associative" or "non-associative learning", "habituation", "sensitisation", "operant" and "classical conditioning", "positive" and "negative reinforcement" and "punishment", amongst others.

Broadly speaking, conventional training theory draws a distinction between "associative" and "non-associative" ways in which horses learn. Associative learning may occur through operant (also sometimes called instrumental) and/or classical conditioning, while habituation and sensitisation are forms of non-associative learning. To avoid the need to reinvent the wheel, let us turn to the internationally renowned head of the Australian Equine Behaviour Centre, Dr Andrew McLean, for a basic introduction to some of these terms, starting with habituation.

> Habituation is the simplest form of equine learning. Nothing happens to reinforce a particular behaviour either positively or negatively: the horse just "becomes used to" something.
>
> (Andrew McLean, *The Truth about Horses*, p. 37)

An example of such habituation would be where a horse becomes used to what it would normally regard as frightening, for instance, the noise of a motorbike. Trainers rely on habituation to desensitise horses to such ostensibly threatening stimuli, especially in the early part of their training. There are also too many trainers who resort to restraints and compulsion to forcefully habituate horses to an overwhelming abundance of certain stimuli that they would normally perceive as threatening. This is known as "flooding".

Sensitisation occurs where the horse learns to become more sensitive to a phenomenon or even the human themself. As a result, the horse responds more readily to the relevant phenomenon or any requests that are made of them by the human. Klaus Ferdinand Hempfling is probably the most well-known horse person who employs this approach.

Classical conditioning is "the means whereby secondary reinforcements are learned by association" (McLean, p. 47). An experiment conducted by the well-known researcher, Ivan Pavlov (1849-1936), into the relationship of salivation and the movements of the stomach in dogs best illustrates this type of training. As part of this experiment a bell was rung at the same time as Pavlov fed his dog, who salivated when they saw the food. With repetition the dog came to associate the food with the bell and salivated as soon as they heard it, irrespective of whether or not they were offered any. This Pavlov referred to as a "conditioned reflex" and called the process of learning it "conditioning". Clicker training is partly based on this approach, the clicker serving as the secondary reinforcement. The primary reinforcement on which any secondary reinforcement occurs normally takes the form of operant conditioning, which McLean describes as the "most important form of training" (McLean, p. 40).

Operant conditioning involves the horse learning that, if they behave in a certain way, they will be rewarded or punished. The reward may take the form of a pleasant experience on its own to encourage the replication of the behaviour rewarded, such as a treat, or one which involves relief from an unpleasant experience, for example, the application of pressure followed by relief from that pressure when the desired behaviour is exhibited. In the former case we refer to positive reinforcement and in the latter negative reinforcement. The aim in both cases is to encourage the replication of the behaviour rewarded.

Punishment, and positive and negative reinforcement are not mutually exclusive and may be used together and in conjunction with classical conditioning with or without further refinements which extend beyond the scope of this discussion.

Punishment

Essentially, punishment involves forcing the horse to undergo an unpleasant experience. Such an experience may take the form of the application of an unpleasant stimulus, such as a shock (referred to as "positive punishment", an oxymoron to many) or the withdrawal of a pleasant stimulus, such as food ("negative punishment"), in order to punish unwanted behaviour. Punishment is what McLean considers to be "the least effective form of learning", firstly because "it mostly does not work, the only exception being where it is applied within one second of the behaviour occurring" (McLean, p. 45). Secondly, "it doesn't allow the horse (or dog or child…) to practise the correct behaviour" (McLean, p. 46).

Staying within the utilitarian framework within which McLean considers punishment, one might also question his conclusion to the effect that punishment has the potential to be effective if applied within one second of the unwanted behaviour occurring. Firstly, the period of one second represents an arbitrary selection. After all, who is to say that this may be true for one horse but not for another?

More importantly though, there is the question of the long-term effect which punishment may have on the horse even if it is applied so promptly as to be effective in eliminating the undesired behaviour (assuming that this does indeed occur, an assumption which is debatable). Surely the repeated use of punishment has the potential to produce a horse whose character is so subdued under the saddle or even on the ground, that the creature is no longer capable of displaying the grace and controlled power that once induced their carer to acquire them? At the other end of the spectrum, could it not also ultimately create a wildly dangerous monster or anything in between?

At this stage we have not even devoted attention to the ethical considerations which any approach to training arguably needs to contend with. For utilitarian reasons alone punishment would therefore appear to be a largely unreliable tool and, as such, one which has no place in any training programme, even one which seeks to compel the horse to behave in a certain way or to refrain from specific behaviour.

Negative reinforcement

Where horses are concerned, "negative reinforcement", which is also sometimes described as the withdrawal of an aversive (a *nice* word for "unpleasant" or "stressful") stimulus, once the desirable behaviour is forthcoming, largely takes the form of "yielding to pressure" (an oxymoron from the horse's perspective in many, if not most, situations in which physical contact is involved). You will find an extensive discussion of this subject in the chapter entitled, *Yielding to Pressure: The Reality of the Myth.*

What should also be noted with regard to negative reinforcement, timing is everything. If the unpleasant stimulus is not removed at exactly the right moment, some form of behaviour may be reinforced other than that which the trainer deems to be desirable.

Positive reinforcement

Where horses are involved, the positive reinforcement reward often takes the form of a treat. Probably the most well-known form of positive reinforcement is clicker training, which combines this form of operant conditioning, usually involving the use of treats, with classical conditioning in its use of a secondary reinforcement (the clicker) ultimately as a replacement for the primary reinforcement (the treat). A further refinement may involve the substitution of the clicker with a more subtle trigger to elicit the conditioned behaviour.

As in the case of negative reinforcement, timing is crucial if positive reinforcement is to serve as an effective approach to horse training. It also involves the risk of training undesirable behaviour where the trainer's timing is off.

Positive or negative reinforcement: practical considerations

Although Andrew McLean contends that negative reinforcement is more effective than its positive variant, there is a growing body of evidence, empirical and anecdotal, which strongly suggests that the opposite is true. An internet search should turn up sufficient evidence to prove the point. To this extent we may conclude that merely from a utilitarian perspective, positive reinforcement is preferable as an effective approach to horse training.

Having said this, anecdotal evidence suggests that the use of treats as a means of positive reinforcement may backfire depending on the horse's response. Anaïs, one of our mares, may serve as an example in this respect. She is highly food-focused, something which anecdotal evidence suggests that she has in common with other orphan foals. Even when the timing was spot on, she became so obsessed with food rewards that she started to beg for treats. It was not that she mugged Vicki (my partner and wife) or myself for food. On the contrary, she made a point of avoiding physical contact while inching as close to the source of treats (she has a superb sense of smell) as possible. Of greater concern though was Anaïs' tendency to reproduce conditioned behaviour of her own volition and to follow this up with a nose in our direction to solicit a reward. Clearly, she is not a horse we were keen on continuing to reward with treats, even though she is a very quick learner. Clicker training was therefore abandoned.

Negative reinforcement: ethical considerations

When ethical considerations are thrown into the mix, it is self-evident that there is no contest. Positive reinforcement does not subject the horse to any physical harm, discomfort or stress. The same cannot be said for negative reinforcement. The proponents of the latter are quick to mention that the ultimate aim of negative reinforcement is to rely on the lightest of aids. This may be true but there is simply no doubt that the path to this goal demands that at the very least the horse must undergo physically unpleasant and stressful experiences. In addition, the presence of video and television cameras at public events featuring the most skilled equestrian practitioners has produced a wealth of incontrovertible evidence which reveals that, even in its most well-intentioned and professional guise, negative reinforcement ultimately relies on physical force or the threat of it.

The proponents of negative reinforcement are quick to argue that it cannot be harmful or stressful to horses, as many, if not most of them, accept it without resistance or evidence of discomfort judging from their "willingness" to work and their positive attitude as evidenced in their bright eye and forward-pricked ears, even in the case of horses cajoled into what should be essentially recreational rather than essential activities (for example, "human" sports such as dressage, jumping, eventing and the like) with the aid of metal and leather restraints and instruments of force which are more appropriate to bondage and discipline sessions (absolutely non-consensual in the case of the horse) than sports. Alternatively, they draw attention to a growing number of examples of horses dutifully performing the most amazing feats at their controller's behest or demonstrating an almost slavish desire to follow their master wherever he might lead them. Indeed, some humans regard such behaviour as an example of a relationship between horse and human which is so close that they are prepared to spend considerable sums of money on attempts (often as frequent as they are futile) to replicate it in their relationship with their own horse.

This is where we may wish to stop and consider a number of possible explanations for the occurrence of signs of the horse's averred acceptance of negative reinforcement, which not only refute those arguments but are also decidedly more plausible than them. In the first place we need to be aware that, with the exception of trauma memory, which is predominantly an involuntary rather than a conscious phenomenon in the species, horses live entirely in the moment and have a capacity to bear adversity which is testimony to their inherent ability to cope with the hardships which nature springs on creatures that were originally designed to live in the wild. Where such hardships are offset by an acceptable (to the horse) level of well-being, the horse accepts them as par for the course, as it were. And it is precisely because horses do accept many of the hardships that we inflict upon them that many humans conclude either that we are justified in doing so and/or that horses do not mind.

The problem with this line of reasoning is that it masks an inexcusable degree of self-delusion and a denial of our own responsibility for the well-being of our horses. It is a denial of such responsibility to the extent that it requires the horse to determine the extent of our responsibility for its well-being rather than that we do this ourselves. In this sense we accept that we will do to the horse whatever they allow us to do to them. But by doing so we are effectively denying our responsibility to set our own standards of well-being for our horses, one which seeks to reduce or eliminate those hardships which our horses tolerate. And it is self-delusional to the extent that we delude ourselves that we do not bear such responsibility.

Alternatively, a more persuasive explanation for the occurrence of signs of the horse's averred acceptance of negative reinforcement may lie in their acquisition of learned helplessness or a similarly debilitating condition which I refer to as stress-induced shut-down.

Pioneered by the American psychologist, Martin Seligman, and based on experiments conducted on dogs in 1967 which would probably be in breach of current bans against animal cruelty, the concept of learned helplessness refers to behaviour on the part of a living creature after it learns that whatever they do, they will not be able to escape from an aversive situation and they consequently give up trying to do so in a new situation (even where they have the ability to do so). In the case of horses trained with the aid of negative reinforcement (whether coupled with punishment or not) this may result in the horse refusing to do anything whatever the aversive treatment meted out to it.

By way of an example, I would like to cite the case of our gelding, Farinelli. In what I prefer to look back on as our "dark days" – that is, a time of ignorance and the cruelty which it both wittingly and unwittingly fostered – this young horse increasingly resisted dressage training for reasons that we and our trainers interpreted as "stubbornness" and "naughtiness". There could be no other explanation surely. After all, everyone admired his glorious loping trot at liberty, especially when he tossed Vicki off his back while warming up for a competition and then crossed three dressage arenas in full regalia minus a rider, drawing gasps of simultaneous shock and admiration from judges and contestants alike. Surely, this was evidence of what he was capable of. One trainer's suggestion was to "whack him", while another's solution took the form of using a whip and spurs to cajole him on. I personally watched the second trainer spend more than twenty minutes doing this while increasing the intensity and violence of her movements, only to be met by a stoic refusal to budge on the part of the graceful gelding. Some time later Farinelli was diagnosed with kissing spine and the penny dropped. Whatever was done to him, he froze and acted as though he could not escape pain, whether it was the pain in his back or that inflicted by the whip and the spurs, yet he was fully capable of doing precisely that by merely throwing off his rider. He has never been ridden since.

Related to this is the condition which I have dubbed stress-induced shut-down. Although I was not fully aware of its significance at the time, when Farinelli was experiencing learned helplessness I noticed that his eyes seemed to glaze over and his glance would be directed firmly within himself even though his eyes stared at the horizon. It was though he had cut himself off from the situation in which he found himself.

Years later the significance of that glazed inward glance became apparent soon after my mare, Pip, came into my life. A Dutch warmblood taken to a fairly advanced intermediate level of dressage in the Netherlands by one or more of her previous seven owners, she had clearly been ridden skew (as evidenced by her grossly dissimilar shoulders and fore-hooves) and against the bit while being pulled into a frame (as testified by the pain in her shoulders and hard crest). Thinking that liberty work might help, I took off all the tack, only to be met by a horse that careered up and down the fence-line in utter panic. Even when working at liberty after settling down a bit, Pip displayed a side to her which began to make sense when put into the perspective created by talk on the part of her previous owner and others who had known the horse, to the effect that she had a predisposition for speed and was not an "easy" horse. While exercising her on the circle, I noticed that she had a tendency to speed up and shut herself off to all contact rather than refuse to trot when she was at liberty to do so. What I realised in Pip's case – thanks in part to my experience with Farinelli – was that she was in pain. Her only way of dealing with it was to do as asked but to speed up and to shut down while doing so. To the outside world she seemed to be compliant and obedient but to anyone who knew her it was clear that there was absolutely no contact or communication between horse and human.

Positive reinforcement: ethical considerations

As positive reinforcement does not seem to inflict any harm on the horse, you may be forgiven for wondering why I am devoting a section on ethical considerations in relation to it. The reason why I have elected to do this lies in the implications which positive reinforcement in general and clicker training, in particular, may have on the relationship between horse and human and, as such, the pursuit of the dream of the two species learning to *dance* together as willing partners.

No matter how physically harmless positive reinforcement may be to the horse, the product of a training regime employing it is conditioned behaviour. This is to say that such behaviour is not the spontaneous expression on the part of a willing horse but rather an automated response to a cue or stimulus. The question that arises in this respect is whether the training and elicitation of such behaviour does not do the horse a psychological disservice in that it deprives them of the ability to express themselves freely, a capability which a horse normally enjoys at liberty in the absence of a controlling human.

Nevertheless, I am aware that the employment of positive reinforcement may help to build bridges between horses and humans, where the relationship between the two species has been undermined by trauma occasioned by humans or otherwise. I know of two examples where this has occurred. In one case a friend in Australia has successfully employed clicker training to enable her to perform basic horse care on a large, powerful gelding whose distrust of humans rendered him potentially dangerous.

In another case a Welsh pony with whom Vicki carried out Equine Touch in a horse refuge centre in Andalusia, Spain, had become very aggressive towards humans as a result of abuse during the financial crisis which engulfed the country, and which saw many horses ill-treated and abandoned. The pony has been receiving clicker training at a facility in Granada, which has finally made it possible for humans to provide him with the care that he requires without fear of being bitten and kicked.

While it is true that positive reinforcement approaches, such as clicker training, do produce conditioned behaviour, it is also clear that a regime which does not employ force or the threat of force, potentially creates the conditions for the development of a relationship of trust between horse and human. Ultimately, such a relationship may make it possible for the human to abandon training which seeks to condition the horse's behaviour, thereby providing the two species with an opportunity to pursue the dream.

Dream or illusion?

You may have read treatises or manuals on operant and classical conditioning which refer to the application of the so-called four quadrants: R+, R-, P+ and P-. These symbols stand for positive and negative reinforcement, and positive and negative punishment respectively. All too often analyses of – and worse, instructions for – training refer to the application of combinations of these symbols. Consequently, the humans involved in such activities become more preoccupied with the application of those symbols as a cause designed to produce a specific effect than their impact on the horse.

When all is said and done, the proof of the pudding that is conventional horse training lies in its eating: its outcomes. The purpose of operant and classical conditioning is to condition the behaviour of the horse. It should therefore come as no surprise to learn that, if such training is effective, the horse will exhibit conditioned behaviour whenever the appropriate cue is given to trigger that behaviour or an aid is applied which achieves precisely that, irrespective of whether or not positive or negative reinforcement has been applied.

So what exactly does this mean? Quite simply, it means that any behaviour which the horse exhibits as a result of such training is anything but spontaneous. It is absolutely not the voluntary expression of a consciously willing partner acting of their own volition but rather a form of conditioned behaviour which has been secured through coercion (in the case of negative reinforcement and/or punishment, flooding or the like, however willing the horse may seem to be) or trick training (where a positive reinforcement approach such as clicker training is employed).

If the dream is to be lived through the attainment of contact, communication and ultimately a true connection between horse and human in their capacity as sentient beings with a will of their own which is so special as to enable them to create a magical symbiosis together as willing partners that is greater than the sum of its parts, then it is clear that the conventional approach to horse training is doomed to fall drastically short of this. Subject to the caveats mentioned in relation to positive reinforcement, at most we may hope to learn how to make a horse move either in response to force or the threat of force, or in the form of conditioned behaviour. And if living the dream is our goal, the outcome can only be a complete and utter illusion.

The path to the dream

As suggested or implied above, the path towards living the dream with our horses passes first and foremost through the human and requires that we develop body and spiritual awareness to establish the basis for it within ourselves. The initial goals, as I see them, are to establish the following with our horses:

1. contact – when we enter our horse's circle of awareness, our horse notices our arrival and clearly shows us this, which opens the channels of communication;
2. communication – we are able to communicate with our horse without resorting to force or the threat of it;
3. connection – we have a close energetical connection with our horse which is based on mutual trust and our presence, which is so authentic, trustworthy and dependable that the horse chooses to be with and be guided by us.

It seems to me that, once we can achieve this without the use of force or the threat of it and depending entirely on our own inner strength, we will be well on the path to living the dream. Only then will true mutually beneficial training be possible but within an entirely different paradigm, one which is situated within the context of the very personal relationship between horse and human. To quote Michael Bevilacqua, "Understanding and trust have nothing to do with training." Even more pertinently, he also notes the following:

The relationship forged through true respect toward another living creature can bring such beautiful, previously unthinkable rewards. However, the same horse will not allow a person other than yourself to simply place a halter on his head. There is a difference between knowing, trusting and being trained and broken.

(Quoted by Nevzorov Haute Ecole on its Facebook page on 8 May 2015)

Within such a paradigm there can be no place for an approach which equates horse training with a software upgrade or which seeks to deny the horse the right to freedom of expression, a right which we claim for ourselves. Instead of pursuing conditioned behaviour and/or resorting to force or the threat of it, training will be geared towards the creation of building blocks for communication, much like the words and structures we acquire when learning a new language. And rather than trying to control our equine friend through an unimaginative, soul-destroying work regime, we will seek to offer guidance, encouragement and support within a context of play inspired by joy. (Is it not time for the term, "work", to be banished from the training vocabulary?)

CONTEMPLATIONS ON RIDING A HORSE

What follows is a series of three articles based on blog posts written while contemplating the prospect of riding my mare, Pip, for the very first time several years after she entered my life.

Riding What?

It was a bit of a toss-up, determining where to start on the question of riding. My instinct tells me that Klaus Ferdinand Hempfling is right: you start with the human and not the horse, for ultimately it is the human that needs to change and to rediscover what it is to be human if they are to be of any value to the horse. On the other hand, the horse already knows how to be a horse and has not lost that knowledge of its species as we have of ours. Yet in the absence of the horse, a human has no need to consider the matter of riding, a realisation which seems to suggest that the horse must nevertheless be mentioned first, for it is the *sine qua non* (without which nothing) of riding. So let us turn to the horse in the first of this series of articles dedicated to the preparations which Pip and I are undertaking towards riding.

What is a horse?
Gosh, what a dumb question! We all know what a horse is, don't we. It is a "solid-hoofed plant-eating domesticated mammal with a flowing mane and tail, used for riding, racing, and to carry and pull loads" (Oxford online dictionary) or a "large animal that is used for riding and for carrying and pulling things" (Merriam-Webster online dictionary). So there you have it. Let us take the common denominator of these definitions from the most authoritative dictionaries in the English language: a horse is a domesticated animal used for riding, and carrying and pulling loads.

76

Which means that, if you did not have any idea what a horse was before you read either of these definitions, once you had, you might only expect to see a horse with bits of metal, rope and/or leather about its body to enable humans to ride it or get it to carry or pull a load. If you want to get to know horses better, you would probably start out by visiting a riding school, where your initiation would start through an interface made up of your bum and the horse's back. Odds are that this is probably how you started out with horses, if you did not grow up in a family that keeps them. But if you did, the chances are pretty good that the bulk of your relationship with a horse has developed through that very same interface.

Don't they come with tack on?
In fact, most people who spend time with horses and have come to learn about them can probably trace much if not most of their knowledge of *equus caballus* back to that interface of bum and back. You learn about the tack you need to keep your bum on the horse's back and the training you require to do the very same while learning how to make the horse do things while your bum is on their back. Indeed, you may even go further and learn about the accommodation, feed and care a horse should have in order to be able to bear your bum on its back.

If you are really keen, you may even learn a bit about the biomechanics of a horse, which will enable you to "train" them to such a high level that you can make them do spectacular moves while your bum is firmly ensconced on their back. Indeed most of us who spend time with horses will probably know of few ways of spending that time with a horse other than with our bum on their back, and if we do manage to find another way, it is usually merely designed to enable us to keep our bum on their back but with greater finesse.

We should therefore be excused if we fail to comprehend how anyone could walk with a horse on a lead in a forest instead of being seated on its back (a lack of comprehension which numerous riders have expressed to Vicki and myself when they have encountered us walking next to Anaïs and Pip in the forest). Indeed, we might even be excused if we have difficulty visualising a horse without tack on its body, a saddle on its back and metal studs on its hooves. Doesn't a horse come with tack and metal studs on it? If you were unfamiliar with the concept of a "horse" and saw an illustration from a highly recommended book on equine biomechanics featuring a horse's leg with a metal stud (also known as a "horseshoe") attached, you might even be forgiven for thinking that.

The light comes on at fifty

This is more or less how horses came into my life as a teenager. I knew nothing about them other than that many of my friends owned one and that every now and then I was given the opportunity to ride one of them. Someone taught me the basics of how to keep my bum on the horse's back when it moved, and how to make it move while my bum was on its back. This stood me in good stead on the odd occasions when a horse bolted under me, although it was not much help the day Gulliver and I encountered a wallaby (a smaller "version" of a kangaroo) in Australia. Good old Gulliver instilled in me the knowledge that a horse is a creature of flight, the lesson being learned the moment he veered out of the path of the *skippy* and I kept on going straight without a horse's back underneath my bum and landed on my head. Fortunately, I was wearing a helmet. I may have been macho in my younger days but I was not comfortable with the idea of dying (let alone "being") stupid.

And so horses drifted in and out of my life as creatures with whom a relationship could be developed through my bum and their back, until I lost interest in about 2002. Yes, I was prepared to help Vicki with our two geldings, Gulliver and Farinelli, when work commitments allowed but I was no longer interested in riding or doing anything else with them or any horse really. I could simply no longer see the point of making another creature do or not do something for me, especially one with whom I did not seem to have much affinity and only really appreciated as another member of our menagerie (we had four dogs and four cats at the time) and fellow earth inhabitant.

It was in the year when I turned fifty, that everything changed. I discovered Nevzorov (and through him Michael Bevilacqua later on) and Klaus Ferdinand Hempfling. In ways peculiar to them these people inspired me to set off on a journey which, amongst other things, has led me to discover horses for what they are and not merely what we humans would like them to be. It is a journey that has revealed what other humans have discovered about horses but more importantly it is one that has allowed me to develop the skills and ability to start learning what horses offer us for discovery about themselves and ultimately what we can discover through them about ourselves.

Horses before humans
In a sense Nevzorov, Bevilacqua and Hempfling (and later Imke Spilker, Frédéric Pignon, Carolyn Resnick, Mark Rashid and Linda Kohanov) made it possible for me to start seeing horses as they are before humans exert their influence over them. It became clear to me that they are exceptionally sociable, seeking safety and security in relationships with other horses both as members of the same equine community and as close friends with another horse in the same herd. They are also creatures that are highly sensitive to and equally perceptive of an array of stimuli that are visible and invisible, audible and inaudible, tangible and intangible, and are capable of responding intuitively to them. In addition, they prefer collaboration and cooperation to the disquieting effects of conflict (with the exception of stallions competing for mares). It has also become clear to me that horses are capable of bonding closely with humans and those in captivity rely on us entirely to have their physical, emotional and other needs met, while acquiescing in or enjoying our guidance. To this extent, but only to this extent, we are the dominant species and, as such, we are challenged to empathise with horses, to be enlightened in our dealings with them, and to empower them, rather than to dominate them for our own selfish purposes.

These perceptions and deductions have since been confirmed by further study, for it is my belief that I should not aspire to riding a creature in the absence of instruments of force – that is, placing my trust in the horse to the extent that I unconditionally put my aging bones at its mercy – without understanding its nature.

Yet there is another aspect which needs to be mentioned, because it explains why of all the animals on the earth, the horse has held an appeal for humans over the centuries beyond its role as a beast of burden which is more widespread and extends to more profound spheres of human endeavour than any other. In the course of time the horse has featured prominently in human politics, religion, sport and imagination as expressed in the arts and iconography, and still does to a significant extent today. At a personal level the horse is also arguably the only animal species with which humans can interact in a way that is capable of generating a nobility and beauty which is greater than the sum created by the two species doing on their own what they might otherwise do best together.

Safe, secure and at home
In his YouTube videos, *Immediate Connecting with Horses: 1* and *2*, Hempfling notes what I feel is so important, that I wish to quote it here. Speaking about the connection he achieves with a horse during his first encounter with it, he states that to get a:

> ... positive response from the horse immediately means that I have to have a kind of unspoken contract with the horse. And this means, for example, that I will do everything not anyhow to hurt you, and I promise you to be on the maximum of peace in whatever I am going to do. I'm promising you that I'm going to take care that I will not be doing anything, not a simple step which is not in accordance with your proper individual growing. I'm the one who has to lead. There is no doubt about it. I have to lead in accordance with the needs and with the nature of the horse: give him safety, give him everything he needs to feel at home.

Whether or not you agree with Hempfling's claim that he manages to connect immediately with every horse that he encounters for the first time – there is evidence that he does with most of the horses he chooses to encounter and evidence is also available to the effect that he fails to do so with a small proportion of the horses that he selects – is utterly irrelevant for our purposes. What is relevant is the essence of what he states, a lesson which Pip has personally been trying to teach me since April 2012 and which she finally managed to do in January 2014 (some of us are hard learners).

That lesson is this: if you truly want to achieve a true, magical connection with your horse on a lasting basis, you will have to do everything in your power to show through your actions that your horse is safe and secure enough with you to be able to relax and be themself, which is simply their way of expressing their trust in you. It is my belief that anyone can make a horse move and some of us are far better doing that than others. The true challenge though lies not in making the horse do something but in the human finding it within themselves to encourage the horse to want to join in the dance with us, to become a willing partner. This, if I correctly understand the Nevzorovs, Bevilacquas and Hempflings of the world and the other guides whom I have cited, is the true goal of training. Yet without that true, magical connection it will be impossible to achieve that goal and without the horse feeling safe, secure and at home with you, they will not be able to trust you and that connection will remain an unattainable aspiration.

So what?
So what does this mean to Pip and me, as we continue our preparations for riding? In a nutshell, it means that before I can even begin to contemplate preparations for riding, Pip needs to be a happy, healthy horse in mind and in body. She needs to feel so safe, secure and at home with me that she will trust me enough to go along with anything that I ask, which she might initially feel is utterly alien and inappropriate, and that she will trust me enough to know that I truly do not seek to ask more of her than she is willing and able to give.

So how can I gauge the progress that we are making in this respect? Simple. Pip shows me. She has shown me that she is healthy. I look at her neck and see that the short, hard muscles which she had when she came into my life have given way to long, loose muscles which give her greater flexibility. My mare's feet have also improved. Not only has her tendon healed but she is now also capable of negotiating the hardest surfaces without any pain or discomfort while barefoot. In addition, she is straighter and more balanced when she stands and walks. Pip now stands square and upright, and when she walks she now overtracks (the toe of her hind foot lands beyond the print of the toe of her fore foot) on both sides instead of only on the left.

The evidence is also discernible in Pip's attitude towards life and me. She is no longer that anxious bundle of nerves she used to be. Instead, she is more self-assured, is moving up the ranks in the herd and is even beginning to challenge Anaïs on occasion. Pip and Anaïs are part of a herd of 18 horses that have been living together relatively uneventfully for some five months now. When Vicki and I arrive at the yard, either or both of us normally call to the horses from the entrance to the horse enclosure and our mares simply come to us. In the past Anaïs used to initiate the action and arrive first. Now it is Pip. In fact, on many occasions she recognises my tread on the pebbles close to the gate before she sees me and often arrives at the entrance before I have even looked around to find her.

Putting Pip on a pedestal
Another example. Vicki has taught Anaïs to stand on a pedestal. For ages I had tried to do the same but every time Pip simply walked off almost shaking her head as if to say, "You're crazy". Caring for Pip while she was having problems with her tendon was a watershed experience for us. Her attitude towards me changed completely. I did not realise just to what extent it had, until I took her to the pedestal, put my foot on it and uttered the cue, "Step", as I had vainly done so many times before, and she lifted her hoof slightly. I then bent down and raised it on to the edge of the pedestal to show her what I meant

and then we tried the whole thing again. This time Pip simply put her foot on the pedestal and turned her head towards me as if to say, "Oh that's what you want? Well, here you are then." I could not believe it.

But more was still to come. A few days later I took Pip to watch Anaïs put both front feet on the pedestal but my mare did not seem to be overly impressed. A week later I discovered why. Asking Pip to put one foot up onto the pedestal and trying not to expect anything, my mare looked at me, turned back to the pedestal and simply stepped up onto it with both front feet. The next time I asked her a week later, she promptly walked right up and over the thing.

Is Pip ready for preparations for riding? I do not think that I am putting her on a pedestal when I say, "I think so". Of course, although I am hoping to start riding Pip next month, I am aware that I may never do so for one reason or another, for instance if she declines to have my bum on her back. At the beginning of April Pip and I will have been together for two years. Next month we will also both celebrate our respective birthdays. She will turn 17 and I will be 57. It is not the youngest age to contemplate a new start and certainly not one which envisages riding without metal in the mouth or on the feet. With the exception of the odd occasion on which Vicki has sat on her for a few minutes at a time in the manège, Pip will not have felt a human bum on her back for a little over two years. I have not had my bum on a horse's back for more than 10 years. There are moments when I suspect that sanity has deserted me. But then a consoling thought comes to me: even though I may never get to ride Pip, it sure is great preparing to do so. For both of us, I think.

To Ride or Not to Ride? This is the Question

Two comments on what I wrote as part of my reflections on the horse in relation to riding have profoundly affected my thoughts in the past few weeks and in doing so have helped create the basis for this article. The first comment came from Peggy on the east coast of Australia and it is this: "if you have a bond with your horse, are kind, considerate and don't ask too much too soon ... that is it in a nutshell". The second was from Jade, who lives at the other end of the continent in Western Australia, and she wrote:

> I have been thinking a lot lately about the horses' pain and riding and through working with a local equine Bowen therapist, I have realised that horses having some degree of muscle soreness or pain is generally accepted as a part of them being ridden. And the more I think about it, the more I realise that I have not come across one regularly ridden horse that does not have pain somewhere in the body, which scares me greatly. Now I'm on the search to see whether there are ways to prevent this.

At first glance these two comments appear to reflect views at opposite ends of the spectrum. More importantly, they seem to imply a need to examine an underlying question whose profundity is all too often glossed over if not simply ignored: *To ride or not to ride?* This is the question.

The old and the new
Peggy is a dear friend who has often commented on the *Horses and Humans* blog and who opened her home to my partner and myself again during a trip to Australia in the past. While we stayed with her, we were again privileged to witness the close bond that she enjoys with her horses and the extent to which they trust her. Older than we are and with vastly more experience of horses, to me Peggy represents a bit of what we humans have lost in our relationship with horses: the older generation's ability to enjoy a no-nonsense, both-feet-firmly-on-the-ground, bullshit-free relationship with horses which is guided by genuine care and concern, albeit based on the assumption that riding is an essential part of that relationship to the extent that it is possible and enjoyable to engage in that activity while treating horses fairly and respectfully.

Jade is a young woman whom I have never met but whose inquiring mind and youthful wisdom stunned me when I first encountered her presence through the *Horses and Humans* blog. So astounded was I that I promptly devoted a post to the story of Jade and her horses, Cisco and Dougie, and the revelations which it elicited within me. Entitled <u>Stillness in the Brumby's Breath</u>, that post serves as an appropriate background to this discussion along with my last post, which essentially deals with a human's awareness of the nature of the horse.

To me Jade represents part of the new generation of horse-loving humans who no longer wish to take everything for granted in their dealings with horses, in particular, the assumption that the driving force of the relationship between our species is the interaction between a horse's back and a human's bum. Jade opens her comment on my previous article with this introductory statement: "I have been following your posts closely lately because I have been contemplating the ethics of asking horses to carry us on their back, amongst other things we ask of them." The question, "To ride or not to ride?", is implicit in this comment. Has anyone you know ever asked themselves this question before placing their buttocks firmly and squarely on a horse's back and assuming that their "equine friend" has undertaken to carry them? Have you? Have I? Is it not a question that we should ask ourselves instead of assuming that our horse wants to carry us or insisting that they have a duty to do so?

Those who say "No"
There are humans I know of who have come to answer the question, "To ride or not to ride?" with a resounding "No". What makes their answer worth listening to is the fact that they include some of the most accomplished horse people of our time, humans who have not only demonstrated their ability to train and ride a horse but who have managed to do so without resorting to instruments of force in order to do so, relying instead on their commitment to developing a close relationship with their equine friends, as part of which the horse

becomes a willing partner rather than a servile subordinate in the interaction between the species.

Alexander Nevzorov used to be one of if not the most proficient horsemen on the planet, capable of helping a thoroughbred stallion and mare to learn and want to perform *haute ecole* (high school dressage) at a level comparable to that of the Spanish School of Riding in Vienna, Austria, the Cadre Noir in Saumur, France, and the Portuguese School of Equestrian Art in Lisbon, Portugal, and doing so with nothing more than a *cordeo* (neck rope) and a twig. Committed to a scientific approach towards understanding the horse and a passionate defender of the species' right to a life devoid of pain and suffering at the hands of humans, Nevzorov advocated riding for no more than ten to fifteen minutes at a time, before eventually concluding that even this compromised a horse's health. He therefore decided to stop riding completely.

In Canada the Nevzorov Haute Ecole's international representative, Michael Bevilacqua, a horseman with, as I understand it, an essentially different approach towards horses, one exhibiting more of an intuitive rather than a scientific bent, has come to a similar conclusion. Unlike Nevzorov, who received extensive classical dressage training before evolving his own horse-friendly approach, Michael Bevilacqua came to horses relatively late in life and had already developed a sensitivity and intuitive style by that stage, enabling him to move much more quickly than most towards developing a force-free, mutually empowering approach towards horses which allowed his equine friends to become willing partners in their dances together with him.

Another one-time Nevzorov Haute Ecole member, Stormy May, has also renounced horse riding. Famous for her release of *Path of the Horse*, a video documentary which has done much to induce many humans to consider a new way of being with horses, Stormy May's story is special in that she used to be a traditional, successful trainer of horses and humans (including other trainers) in what passed for the art of dressage at competition level using a full array of instruments of force, metal and otherwise.

The burden of riding

So why have these humans, who have not only played such an exceptional role in helping others discover a new, horse-friendly way of being and interacting with humans, but have also demonstrated their own proficiency in helping horses to become willing partners in their own training, decided to abandon riding? Much of the answer to this question is to be found in what they have discovered about the effects of riding on the horse and the tools employed to facilitate that pastime, such as bits, bitless head gear, saddles and various other instruments of force. Another part is to be found in the mental and physical condition of the horse, and the posture which they are forced to adopt when a human climbs on their back.

Bits

Over the years various experiments and studies have been carried out by different individuals and organisations into the impact of using common riding equipment such as bits, bitless head gear and saddles. For instance, Robert Cook, PhD., a graduate of the Royal Veterinary College in London, United Kingdom and Professor of Surgery Emeritus at Tufts University, Massachusetts in the United States of America, is a veterinarian who has extensively researched the carnage caused by bits over the years and has developed his own version of a bitless bridle to address his findings. You can read more about his work by visiting his website here (http://www.bitlessbridle.com), where you will also have access to the numerous articles which he has written on the subject, including a paper entitled *A Method for Measuring Bit-Induced Pain and Distress in the Ridden Horse*, which he presented at the Ninth International Equitation Science Conference in July 2013 (see http://www.bitlessbridle.com/MEASURING%20BIT-INDUCED%20PAIN2013.pdf.

The Nevzorov Haute Ecole Research Centre is another organisation which has overseen studies by medical professionals into the effects of bits. One such study involved an experiment into the use of force applied by drawing on the reins or jerking them using a snaffle and a curb bit and featuring three different individuals: a 13-year-old boy, a 23-year-old woman, and a 43-year-old man. The experiment found that the following force was exerted **per square centimetre** of the horse's mouth in contact with the bit:

- 50 kg to 100 kg when the reins were drawn (not pulled);
- 180 kg to 220 kg when the reins were jerked with average force;
- more than 300 kg in the case of a strong jerk.

Not much in the way of imagination is required to picture the impact of such force on the sensitive surface of a horse's mouth. You can find more information about this type of research in Alexander Nevzorov's book, *The Horse Crucified and Risen*.

Bitless

Nevzorov has also written about the effects of using bitless head gear, such as a hackamore, side-pull, bosal, cavesson, or Parelli or other brand of rope halter. You can find more information on this in the anthology produced by Nevzorov Haute Ecole and edited by Lydia Nevzorova entitled *Equestrian Sport: Secrets of the "Art"*.

Saddles

Stormy May has studied some of the work carried out by professionals, such as the saddle-fitting expert, Dr Joyce Harman. A number of studies have been conducted into the effects of riding on a horse's back. Stormy May presents the findings of some of the more pertinent ones in Chapter 3 of her book, *The Path of the Horse: From Competition to Compassion* and quotes Harman's conclusion to the effect that "Pressures that exceed 0.75 psi will close down the blood flow in the arterial capillary bed" of the horse's back, because that is the highest blood pressure found in that area. The best saddles that Harman found in her study were graded at 1.93 psi, which is more than twice the pressure required to cut off the blood flow in the capillaries of the back. According to Harman, studies of canine and human muscles have revealed that sustained pressure of a mere 0.68 psi for over two hours can cause significant superficial tissue damage as well.

Of course, saddle pressure does not only manifest itself on the surface of the horse's back. It is actually transferred through the muscles to the bony structures. Stormy May quotes Harman as stating that, "There is surgical evidence in human medicine that subcutaneous necrosis [the death of cells] begins closer to the bone before cutaneous redness and ulceration is seen". Transposed to the equine condition, this means that white spots or tender swelling in the saddle area are the end results of a long process of shallow and deep tissue destruction.

Interestingly enough, the effects of saddle stress need not be confined to the saddle area. A poor-fitting saddle may cause pain in the shoulder, withers and lumbar region but the effects may even manifest themselves as pain in the neck. If a horse hollows its back to escape discomfort or pain in the saddle area, there is a very good chance that it will suffer pain in, amongst other places, the brachiocephalicus muscle, that thick, long muscle that runs along the lower part of the neck up to the atlas vertebra at the poll.

Other instruments of force

Not much imagination is required to understand the use and effects of other instruments of force, such as spurs, whips and the numerous physical restraints and devices which humans have invented to compel the horse to do what they want or to prevent the horse from doing what they wish to do. They simply have no place in any healthy relationship between horses and humans.

Physical condition

If a horse is to carry themself properly, they need to be physically fit enough to carry itself. To carry a human a horse also needs to be fit and strong enough to carry the additional weight and put up with its movements, and to achieve a posture that will facilitate this (see *Posture* below). If I would like to ride Pip, the very least I need to do is to ensure that she is healthy, that her feet and teeth are properly looked after, that she develops appropriate musculature and flexibility, that she walks straight and is able to carry herself. This is a prerequisite for a physically healthy life in herself and, as such, must come before any contemplation of riding. It is simply what you would do if you care for your equine friend.

Expecting Pip to carry me if she is physically unable to do so comfortably, would be tantamount to knowingly and wittingly deciding to inflict pain on my horse every time I climb on her back. Would I do this to a friend I claim I love? The situation is made more difficult by the fact that Pip has suffered severe tissue damage during her life, if the large white marks on her withers are anything to go by. Will she be able to carry me without hurting herself?

Mental condition
There is much talk of sports horses being bred to have the keen temperament which is required for top sport, with the result that they are edgy, nervous and easily excitable. To a certain extent this is true. To a large extent it is an apology for the very conditions that humans force sports horses to live in, which are ultimately largely responsible for that very nature. Many if not most sports horses are deprived of the opportunity to live like a horse, being permanently stabled with their only respite from full-time imprisonment in a small cell-cum-toilet (also known as a "stable") being a few hours of training or movement in a walker each day.

Trainers such as Nevzorov, Bevilacqua and Klaus Ferdinand Hempfling have shown that it is quite possible to train horses to perform supremely difficult physical feats without reducing them to potentially dangerous bundles of anxiety. Pip was trained and competed up to a fairly high intermediate level in the Netherlands, which is another way of saying that for many years she was chased into the bit while largely off-balance and having her neck painfully bent as her head was pulled towards her chest in what passes for dressage in that country. The result was a mental condition that reflected the physical trauma of riding. Utterly insecure and unsure of herself, she used to be an inconsolably anxious mess when divested of the physical trappings of horse-human contact that she was accustomed to and used to be prone to seeking escape in blind speed whenever she felt remotely threatened. In addition, although she has not really been ridden for more than two years now and has no pain in her shoulders, she still goes through the motions of nervously nipping when I stoop to pick up her front feet, especially on the right, where she used to place the bulk of her weight.

Will Pip be mentally prepared to accept me on her back? More importantly, will she be willing to do so? I have absolutely no idea. What I do know is that I must be prepared for the fact that she will not.

Posture

A horse carries most of their weight on their front legs. Without a human on their back, this does not represent too much of a problem. Put a human on their back and they will start to carry more weight on their front legs and their shoulders than what they can comfortably support. And if that human is unable to synchronise with the horse's movements, the situation will be immensely exacerbated and the horse will suffer more.

It is for this reason that classical dressage was developed. The theory is that by training horse and human, it will be possible for the rider to learn to synchronise their movements with the horse while simultaneously helping the horse to raise the base of their chest and to bring their hind legs further underneath their body, thereby shifting the centre of gravity more towards the rear to redistribute the weight of horse and human more evenly over their feet. The process is often called self-collection or self-carriage (the horse collects and carries itself), although Nevzorov Haute Ecole prefers the term, "natural collection", and if it is done properly it should start from the rear and move to the front arguably leaving the head to find its own position.

As Nevzorov, Bevilacqua and Hempfling have shown, this requires training which allows the horse to seek the posture of collection rather than have the human force the horse into a frame. As such, it is very different from what you will see at dressage competitions at all levels, where the horse is essentially pulled into a frame and ridden into the bit, somewhat like accelerating a car with the brakes on. It is not for nothing that the FEI (the supreme body of equestrian sport) insists that riders use double bridles on their horses at the higher levels of competition. The awesome leverage which those devices employ makes it possible for humans to exert great pressure on the horse's head with a minimum of effort. Remove those instruments of force and you will see very few humans who are capable of riding their horses in self-collection. Indeed, if self-carriage were to become the criterion by which dressage is judged, it is likely that equestrian sport as we know it would not survive in the absence of enough humans capable of helping a horse achieve it.

Personal proof

At the time of writing my partner and I were performing Equine Touch on horses as part of our final case studies en route to becoming practitioners. By the time we qualified we had performed 120 Equine Touch sessions, excluding the many other horses that we have had the privilege of helping without doing so for the purposes of our studies.

When I view the detailed case notes that I have taken for all of those Equine Touch sessions, it is difficult not to conclude that riding inflicts pain on horses in most cases. An Equine Touch session does not involve a human coming in and carrying out a treatment on a horse. It is an interactive session during which we feel and watch the horse, learning from the animal just how they feel and respond to what we are doing.

I have performed Equine Touch on stallions, mares and geldings of a variety of breeds from calm Shetland ponies to stressed 18-hand warmblood sports horses involved in a diversity of activities from recreational riding to jumping and classical dressage. In the vast majority of cases the horse has shown me that they are in pain, often in the back and/or withers but predominantly in the neck and/or shoulders. I have also tried to help owners help their horses by suggesting that they get the hooves, teeth and saddles tended to. Many have done so. Others have not. Yet even where these potential problem areas are eliminated, the pain frequently returns after every ride.

Concealing the evidence

Horses excel when it comes to concealing pain or rather learning to cope with it. If they are generally treated fairly by a caring human, they are more likely to tolerate the discomfort when it occurs. Others become passive victims acquiring the learned helplessness associated with that condition. Still others resist but this is usually a one-way street to annihilation, once they are classed as "dangerous".

Yes, it may be true that in the case of sports horses we try and stretch the animal to achieve the next level. After all, this is what we humans do when we engage in sport. I am not against horses being involved in sport. Many enjoy it. But really, should I not be asking myself whether I have the right to inflict pain on my horse in pursuit of a sport that I have chosen to indulge in, through which my ego and wallet may benefit and in relation to which my horse has absolutely no choice?

Really nice, friendly humans

So what about the humans? Surely they must be monsters, if they regularly inflict pain on the creatures they claim to love? Absolutely not! At the risk of sounding downright condescending, my experience is that, with the exception of the odd horse dealer whom I have had to contend with, the owners of the horses on which I have performed Equine Touch are really nice, friendly humans who, on the whole, want the best for their horses.

So why do I regularly end up performing Equine Touch on horses that are ridden into pain every week? Why do I regularly see horses being ridden that do not have the musculature and general physical condition to support the demands being made of them or whose hooves are in such a terrible state that it is simply a question of time before they start to experience issues in other parts of their body if they have not begun to do so already? What is it that makes a really nice, friendly human do this to the horse they claim to love?

A large part of the answer lies in ignorance. The vast majority of horse owners or riders simply are not aware of the nature of the beast that they ride. Inherent in that ignorance is the dark truth that we humans have been accepting the abnormal in our horses as quite normal for far too long. "Oh, my horse usually does that...." "Yes, my horse can be a bit naughty...." "No, it's just that my horse is normally sensitive around the poll...." "Yes, my horse always shies away from the bridle...." "Oh, my horse usually nips when I tighten the girth...." Sound familiar?

Of methods, techniques, devices and other madness
So what is to be done, if anything? At times such as this one may be tempted to look for solutions in the form of methods, techniques, devices and anything else resembling madness. If all of them are merely designed to cause the horse to do something rather than elicit our equine friend's commitment to being part of the solution, we may want to give that avenue a miss.

Naturally, we may then be tempted to consider the approaches adopted by those we respect for recognising the horse's innate ability to be a partner rather than a pawn. Should we look for guidance to Mark Rashid who rides with a bit and a Western saddle responsible for pressure way in excess of what is required to close down the blood flow in a horse's back, yet who is probably more sensitive to his horse's needs than most? What about Hempfling, who rides bitless with a cavesson and a loose rein but who trains in a picadero of 11-15 metres by 11-15 metres and who insists that the only way forward is that of destiny, his? Perhaps we should be emulating Nevzorov, who once vociferously castigated anyone for relying on any equipment other than a *cordeo* and a twig, and a training area smaller than a sizeable church? Or should we be sitting at the feet of Friendship Training founder, Chuck Mintzlaff, who condemns Bevilacqua for being just another Nevzorov lackey who relies on

94

equipment and a confined space whereas he can do without either, albeit without providing an answer to the question begged as to just how he hopes to help a horse collect themself enough to support a rider in trot and canter without compromising their health?

Stormy May suggests an alternative to everything and all. For this reason it is worth quoting her extensively:

> Now the problem with riding has been detailed, let's look at possible solutions. First, we must understand why we want to ride a horse. If the answers include, "it's fun" "I want to compete" or "it's good exercise" then the previous information will have little or no impact on what you do and the current horse world will give you plenty of support in pursuing your goals. If your answers sound more like, "I love horses" "I want to learn how to have a good relationship with my horse" or even "I think horses might have something to teach me" then it's likely you've already started to look for alternatives to the traditional horse world.
>
> (*Path of the Horse*, p. 33)

It is in the eye

And just what do those alternatives entail? Again, Stormy May suggests an answer to this question:

> The solution has to begin with the premise that the horse knows her own mind, and in any matter regarding her behaviour, she is the authority. Horses don't have a spoken language we can understand but they do have a language we can learn. It is a language of physiology and movement. Once we spend enough time letting go of what we think we know about horses, we leave space for "what is" to reveal itself.
>
> (*Path of the Horse*, p. 33)

Although this statement is essentially true, there is one caveat that must be mentioned. Horses may suffer from trauma-induced muscle memory, which is another way of saying that a past trauma may have induced a physical response in the horse which is still evident in its behaviour even though the original condition that triggered it may have long since healed. My Pip's shoulder sensitivity is a classic example of this.

In essence, though, the horse does point the way forward by communicating with us and an understanding of their language is essential, if we wish to understand our equine friends. Unfortunately, it is not quite as simple as some suggest. For example ears back may mean different things in varying contexts. This is a bit like a human's use of the word "good". Does it always mean *good*? What about "Good, let's do it."? Or "Oh, he's good alright" when talking about a warmonger who has just invaded two countries and legitimised torture in his own? Not to mention "When she's bad, she's very good". In a word, context is everything.

Context is no less significant in the way of the horse. Ears back may mean "I am pissed off". Yet it could also mean "I am dozing" or "I am concentrating". Other aspects of the horse's body language and the context of your relationship with your equine friend will provide the clues as to its intended meaning. Nevertheless, if there is a single beacon which can point you in the direction of properly understanding your horse's language of "physiology and movement", it is likely to be the eye. In a nutshell, if it is hard and unyielding, you have a problem but, if it is soft and yielding, you are on target.

To ride or not to ride?
Vicki and I have had numerous discussions – many of them heated – about methods, techniques, devices and the approaches advanced by the gurus we turn to at times for guidance. If I have learned anything from those debates, it is that, while some of those gizmos lend themselves to abuse, it is also possible for someone riding with a bit in the horse's mouth and a saddle on their back to be kinder and more sensitive to their mount than a well-meaning but clueless rider who bounces around on a horse's naked back while clinging to a cordeo wrapped tightly around their upper neck.

Having said this, it has become abundantly clear to me that riding inherently poses a potential danger to the horse's physical and mental well-being. For this reason I believe that any path towards riding must include contemplation of the question, "To ride or not to ride?". The only creature that can answer this question in such a way that we will know that riding is entirely acceptable to our equine friend is neither you nor I but the horse. For this reason I have decided to approach my preparations for riding Pip on this basis: I will not ride her, until and unless she makes it clear that this is entirely acceptable to her. How will I know? The answer will be in her eye.

To Ride or Not to Ride: Is This Really the Question?

In my last article I posed the question, *To ride or not to ride?*, and stated quite emphatically that this was not only the question, but the one all of us who are contemplating riding a horse should seriously ask ourselves before venturing onto the back of a creature whom we claim to love as a good friend. As the debate got underway two things happened which have since caused me to reconsider whether it is indeed the question that we should be asking ourselves. Perhaps there is a more fundamental issue at stake, one which I had ignored. Then Michael Bevilacqua commented and soon I knew what it was. I would like to deal with that issue now.

So what happened?

First of all, there were comments on the previous article when it was published on the *Horses and Humans* blog, many or most of which, if not all, are profound. Let me deal with some of the points made, if only because they are so pertinent and valid in the light of the issues at stake.

Secondly, there was Pip. My mare decided to make a comment of her own on my contemplation of the question as to whether I should ride her or not. It was a comment which has been decidedly challenging, enough to warrant a re-examination of the question, *To ride or not to ride?*, to the extent that it caused me to question whether the very question itself was not completely off target. Pip's comment too I would like to share with you.

The science

It is interesting to note that only one of the comments questioned the scientific knowledge that we have at our disposal when it comes to determining whether riding is hazardous to the horse. Kelly writes the following:

> I used to earn a living by taking young people out hiking in the wilderness. In the course of this full time work I weighed around 58kg and regularly carried back packs in the range of 20-25kg. The packs were carried for long periods of time, day in day out.
>
> I know I am not a horse, but humans have the same structural make up of cells and blood vessels as horses. So why did I not suffer any pressure damage to my shoulder muscles?

On the face of it this question seems to concern the human shoulders. The context within which it is situated, however, suggests otherwise, for it is introduced as follows: "When the study of the pressure exerted by a saddle and rider are discussed, and how this pressure cuts off capillary blood circulation and starts cellular death in the muscles, the following question arises in me". Put another way, you might restate the question in the light of its context as follows: "If I didn't suffer any pressure damage to my shoulder muscles, how could the pressure exerted by a saddle and rider inflict such injury on a horse?", which is of course as legitimate a question, as the one Kelly actually poses.

Human shoulders and equine backs

As I understand it, a human finds it easiest to carry a load on the shoulders, because it is not merely borne by those body parts but by the entire upright skeletal frame with the exception of the head and neck, albeit that the shoulders and to a lesser but significant extent the back and chest bear the brunt of it. Personally, I would nevertheless be very surprised to hear that any human would not suffer pressure injury to their shoulder muscles when carrying that amount of weight for a prolonged period of time. While I may not be crippled by carrying my lightweight video camera in a small rucksack on my back while on holiday, I definitely notice that I have been carrying it when I remove it. Perhaps this is just another way of asking how much injury do you need to suffer before you experience pain. Of course, once the source of discomfort is permanently removed, the body has a chance to recover and any pain, however slight, becomes a distant memory. If she could speak, Pip might corroborate this based on her experience of two years without being ridden regularly following a history during which she felt pressure on her withers injurious enough to leave vivid scars.

Naturally, a horse's back is a very different body part and is designed primarily to carry the abdominal barrel and part of the thoracic cavity, and to transfer the dynamic energy produced by the hindquarters to the forequarters to facilitate movement. Any vet worth their oats will candidly tell you that the horse's back was never designed to carry weight on top of it and that includes the two-legged variety. One of the reasons for this is that, unlike a human's shoulders, an equine back has no support structure below it. In addition, it is proportionately long, which means that it is more susceptible to sagging, much like a long plank serving as a makeshift bridge across a stream. Then there is the fact that, although the forelegs carry the bulk of the horse's weight, their bony structures are not directly connected to the spine. Instead, that weight is carried in a veritable sling of soft tissue (muscles, ligaments, tendons and so forth) supported on either side by the forelegs. By this stage you would be quite right to conclude that human shoulders are proportionately far stronger than equine backs.

Helping the horse support the human
This is also the reason why the two main styles of riding in the equestrian world – "Western" and "classical" or "English" – seek to help the horse support the human by espousing a mode of riding which tries to avoid hollowing the back. Western riding seeks to do this by keeping the head relatively low at the end of a straight neck. This has the effect of stretching (that is, relaxing) the back muscles, while engaging their abdominal counterparts. The classical tradition tries to achieve the same by encouraging the horse to step further under their body, thereby seeking to stretch the back muscles from the hindquarters. At the same time the horse is supposed to raise the base of their neck thereby shifting their centre of gravity (and hence more of its weight) towards the rear, which would also have the

effect of causing the horse to bend their head down at the poll in order to maintain their balance, lengthening the back muscles from the front at the same time. The advantage of the classical tradition is that the weight is spread more evenly over all of the legs rather than predominantly on the forequarters, as is the case with Western riding.

The only way either "solution" can "work" is if the horse carries themself, as opposed to being "carried" by the rider with the aid of a combination of instruments of force and restraint. In the classical tradition this is what is known as self-collection or self-carriage and what Michael Bevilacqua refers to as "natural collection". It represents a form of movement which is safest – this is not the same as injury-free – for the horse when ridden. Unfortunately, it is also something which is quite rare to find in the classical tradition and virtually impossible at what passes for the summit of equestrian endeavours at the Olympic Games, the World Equestrian Games and other similarly saddening gatherings. You will know it when the instruments of force and restraint are abandoned and you see the horse carry themself. I know of only three public figures who have shown that they are capable of helping a horse do just this: Alexander Nevzorov, Michael Bevilacqua and Klaus Ferdinand Hempfling.

Throwing off the tack
Referring to Alexander Nevzorov, Lina has this to say and it is worth quoting her in full in order to illustrate the point:

> To me it was obvious that the horses in the videos in which he rode with only the cordeo, were the same horses he had used a bridle and bits on previously. I have seen many people who have trained their horses the "traditional" way if you will... with saddles and bridles, be able to work beautifully with their horses bareback and with a halter or just a rope (cordeo) around their neck. They already knew the movements. I can do this to some extent myself with my own trail horses, as can a few of my fellow trail riders – these are not riders who compete in any way shape or form, or do haute ecole, but simply, they have ridden their horses in saddles and bridles

and can then take it all off and the horses know the commands because they come from trust, the seat, the legs, the intention, etc. etc.

It may be true that Alexander Nevzorov trained his horses the traditional way first. It may also be true that Michael Bevilacqua did so as well, as did Hempfling with Ferdinand, that graceful Lipizzaner that dances with him in a video which has garnered more viewings than probably any other YouTube video on the subject. It may also be true that Lina has seen many people "able to work beautifully with their horses bareback and with a halter or just a rope (cordeo) around their neck". The question though is not whether the humans are capable of doing this but whether the horses can carry themselves in natural collection when the tack is thrown off and instruments of force and restraint are abandoned.

A quick search of YouTube will soon reveal that there are very few horses that are capable of carrying themselves in natural collection when the tack is thrown off and they are no longer held together in a frame. This should not be surprising, if one notes that it is possible to score 92.3% at an FEI World Cup Dressage show (the very summit of equestrian prowess, so we are led to believe) on a horse that is not even being ridden in self-collection with all of the tack on! Indeed, for much of the time they are ridden behind the bit (the bit is behind an imaginary vertical line from the poll down), with the crest of the neck as their highest point rather than the poll and hind legs which barely reach underneath the body in trot. Now take away the tack and ask yourself whether the "beauty" of what is not even natural collection will not collapse like a house of cards.

The bottom line
So is riding really detrimental to the horse? Michael Bevilacqua is emphatic: "There is no question about riding a horse being bad for a horse." Yet he used to ride in the past, just as Nevzorov did, albeit only in natural collection and for brief periods at a time, once he had reached a certain level of awareness. In addition, he also quite candidly states the following:

I still support and encourage people, even if their only major decision, is to use a bitless bridle. 2013 was my last seminar, and, yet, it was like a chapter from the past of NHE [Nevzorov Haute Ecole]. Riding was still possible, if only in natural collection.

Jade has also encountered evidence that riding can be physically detrimental to a horse. She proposes a need for further research, contemplation and greater responsibility on the part of riders:

The first thing that comes to mind is that there needs to be more unbiased scientific research into the effects of riding on the horse. Both short-term and long-term, all kinds of riding styles, tackless v with tack, durations of ride etc. Another thing to research would be the effects of starting the horse later in life, i.e. when completely mature. And whether this makes a difference when it comes to riding. Hopefully, this would lead to a more responsible approach to riding for people who still think that it is a necessary part of the horse-human relationship.

The bottom line is that we already know from the research that has already been conducted that riding not only has the potential to be detrimental to the horse but that it can also inflict permanent injury. Although the mental anguish involved can be extreme, here I would like to confine my comments to the physical. Again, evidence suggests that, while riding in natural collection without instruments of pain for relatively brief periods at a time may place some physical strain on the horse, it is unlikely to cause harm. Having said that, I would again like to note that it is possible for an accomplished rider to ride a horse with a fairly harsh bit in natural collection on a loose rein (which of course begs the question as to why one would use a bit in the first place) while inflicting far less discomfort than someone riding with nothing more than a neck ring (cordeo) careering around with the horse's head up in the air, its back hollow and the neck rope collected around its throat.

Survival and learned helplessness
So what about Gary's legitimate query:

> Widely respected horsemen such as Mark Rashid, (in spite of his continued use of the bit) show enormous kindness and consideration for the welfare and well-being of their horses. And yet as a "working cowboy" he has spent on many occasions, either working cattle or running a "dude ranch", very long hours in the saddle.......is that an unforgivable way to behave from a man so "in tune" with horses? Do his horses back away in obvious disapproval when he approaches them with a saddle after remembering that "really long ride" yesterday? I think not. I would be interested to know his view on this subject....

I would not wish to comment on Mark Rashid's approach to riding or that of his horses, even if I felt competent to do so, which I do not. Yet I do not believe that his view on the subject is quite as relevant as that of the horse. The urge to survive is instinctive in the horse and their ability to do so is legendary. Domesticated horses employ an array of techniques to survive their humans' attention including flight, fight and learned helplessness. In many, if not most cases they are not aware of a regime of care and riding other than that which they are accustomed to and so they learn to survive it, even if this means shutting down and doing all that is required of them without protest. You will see it in the eye. In extreme cases the light has gone out. The spirit is dead.

Riding is potentially harmful physically but....
Of course, the physical is not the only dimension of the horse. Mental, emotional and some would even argue, spiritual dimensions are also common to the horse. The challenge of being ridden in natural collection for relatively brief periods at a time may challenge the horse physically and perhaps even cause some minor stress. Penka asks:

> At the same time, Olympic Athletes need good trainers to help them push the limits and challenge the perceptions of what they are capable of? Can this be the case with horses? We probably don't need to be on their backs to do that....

Yet even if we are on their backs when we do that, could it not be that the horse may derive some benefit from such contact with a human within the mental, emotional or spiritual dimension? Perhaps this is what Geerteke is suggesting when she writes the following:

> What if "riding" is part of horse's wish to become aware? What if by denying horse's wish to be ridden human denies horse to evolve? Would that in the core not be an equally cruel act as riding a horse that does NOT wish to be ridden?

> And would it not be almost a natural consequence that disease occurring in human when not listening to its inner voice will also occur in horse when horse is not being listened to its inner voice?

These questions are challenging especially when viewed within the context of the relationship between horses and humans over the centuries. The species have gravitated towards each other in a symbiosis which has encompassed so many different spheres of interaction, including culture, work, sport, religion, health care and entertainment to mention a few. Those who have attended courses with Klaus Ferdinand Hempfling will be aware of the idea of a horse and a human complementing each other to produce a transfigured entity – most visibly expressed in the horse bearing the human – whose combined power and beauty are greater than the sum of its parts. Nowadays horses depend upon humans for their very survival, even in the wild. Conversely though, a growing number of humans are beginning to discover that, if they are to survive as humans and not merely as blighted parodies of the species, horses have much to teach them. Perhaps riding may to some extent constitute part of the process whereby horses and humans derive benefits from each other which extend beyond the physical dimension.

Doubts

To ride or not to ride? The question is challenging if you are open to asking it. Many of us would like to ride but we have doubts about whether we should. Here are a few which some of our readers have expressed.

Penka:

> I also think that we do it with good intentions and we feel that
> we have fulfilling relationships with our horses. They are
> probably ("definitely") more fulfilling for us then for the horse
> and deep down we know that the feeling can be better if truly
> reciprocated... Yet, is this any worse than the parent
> projecting his ideas or life principles on the child? The
> rationale is obvious – good intentions, no major harm, should
> help, I know it better...

I know someone who feels it is okay to use a little bit of force with her horse, if your intentions are honourable, for instance, if you have just mounted your horse but they do not want to move forward. A tug or a smack accompanied by verbal encouragement such as "Come on. Let's go. Now!", much as you might do with a small child (so I am told, which I have to rely on, as I have never had one of my own). My response takes the form of a question: Why should the horse have to move forward with you on their back (or whatever else you are trying to force the horse to do)? Indeed, what gives a human the right to force a horse to do anything? Having said that, there are moments when one simply has to urge a horse to do something, for instance if their health and well-being depend on it. My experience though is that a horse tends to pick up on urgency in the energy one radiates and then responds accordingly, especially if the horse is one with whom you have a close relationship.

Susan:

> I am thankful to all those who have alerted us to the physical
> consequences of being careless and uncaring about our
> horses' backs and bodies, and as a result of their research I
> now ride less frequently and for much shorter periods, and do
> a lot of ground work and play and gymnasticising to help my
> horse feel fitter and more supple, just like yoga helps my not-
> so-young body, so that his energy and enthusiasm might meet
> with mine and give us the pleasure of going out and about
> together without my feeling the compulsion to push him or
> force him where no horse would willingly care to go....

Noble sentiments, yet Susan immediately questions them: "Is this a cop-out on my part? Am I kidding myself just the same way as those who believe in *rollkur* are able to kid themselves that 'it's OK'?" Why question them?

Gary:

> My feeling (OK my imaginative speculation) is that it often comes down to the specific combination of horse and rider and were it possible to interview all horses on the subject there would be just as many who said they enjoyed carrying their rider and felt no ill effects as there would be horses complaining about a sore back and associated ailments. Yes, it could be just wishful thinking on my part as on balance I would like to ride. For the moment as you can gather from this comment, I am sitting on the fence....

I read this and thought: this is as honest as it gets.

Something also niggled at me when I read these comments. To ride or not to ride? Is this really the question?

So which way to go?

To ride or not to ride? If this is the question, what should we do? Which way should we go? Three people came up with an answer which renders the horse's response paramount, albeit inevitably only through the human's interpretation of that response.

Jade:

> The second thing that comes to mind is that, although this can be an extensive and difficult topic, the basis of it is very simple. Go and ask your equine partner. In the end, it's always going to be about the relationship and doing what works for the individual horse-human partnership.

Glenn:

> The TRONTR [To Ride or Not to Ride] question has been on my mind for a while and a few years back I wrote this. Simple

question with no clear cut answer apart from listening to one's inner, intuitive voice, and knowing your horse.

Now I would add, "Listen to your horse, and yourself, and if all is good then get on with it".

Kelly:

The other day, in my mind, Jasper showed me clearly that he was ok with it all. He walked at liberty with me out of the paddock and away from his herd of 12 horses, he walked with me across the front lawn and loaded at liberty onto the truck. Whenever we load up on the truck the simple fact is that we are going riding. I am not trying to justify whether it is right or wrong to ride, each person will find their own way with this and come to their own conclusion, but I am saying – let us not beat ourselves up too much about it all. There are many shades of grey, and only you and your horse will know what is right or wrong in that moment.

Pip's comment

While I was working on my last post, something happened which caused me to doubt part of what I had written. For some weeks I had been working with her to help her prepare her body for the time when I felt it would be alright to pop the question: To ride or not to ride? Would she allow me? As usual, I tried to vary our activities, yet always seemed to be focusing on the goal of riding.

Then Pip commented. Initially, I did not hear her. Pip is not like Anaïs. When Vicki's mare comments, she raises herself majestically upright like a totem pole to impress upon one the folly of messing with close to 600 kg of perpendicular horse. It is impossible not to hear Anaïs when she comments. I tend to listen very quickly. More importantly, I have become very adept at avoiding situations when she may feel a need to comment.

Pip, on the other hand, is the introspective type. She turns inward and closes down communication. In the early days of our relationship I thought that Anaïs was the more difficult horse to deal with but she is not. In fact, she is a big pussy cat. Because she is so expressive, it is much easier to find a way to ensure that those big brown eyes remain as soft as butter. Shutting me out, Pip makes far greater demands of me and I have to dig very deep to re-establish contact with her.

So what was Pip's comment. As I understand it, she was telling me that I had become so focused on this question of riding, that the bossy little man within me had become so insistent on his riding agenda that he was beginning to lose sight of the horse in front of him and the relationship that he wants with that horse. I was ashamed.

A break

Fortunately, a break had been planned. Vicki and I managed to find cheap tickets to the Algarve in southern Portugal (I just love the language, although I can only understand one word of it: *obrigado* – thank you), so we headed there to celebrate my birthday. It is a lovely part of the world with relatively few people, except during the summer when the population triples.

The break created the distance from Pip and the demands of work which I needed to assess what I had been doing with my horse and to re-evaluate my relationship with her. To ride or not to ride? Is it indeed the question? Or was there not something more important at stake? Upon our return to Holland, I felt the answer. I knew and know what kind of human I want to be with Pip and, if that means that riding may be ruled out, so be it. And the moment I let go of the question of to ride or not, Pip and I started to have fun again and we celebrated her birthday soon after our return, reconnected once more.

No, I have not abandoned the prospect of Pip allowing me to ride. We are still doing exercises together which help her to carry herself but the goal of riding no longer dictates the nature of my interaction with Pip. If I ever ride her, this will occur as something incidental to the essence of our mutual enjoyment of each other's company.

The question has to do with the human, not the horse

A little over a week after our return from the Algarve, Michael Bevilacqua's comment arrived. I read it and then reread it the next day. Suddenly I knew how to formulate what I had come to feel intuitively with Pip. This quote from Michael helped:

> There is no question about riding a horse being bad for a horse. However, the question remains about riding – and, subsequently, it has nothing to do with the horse but the people.

We may be tempted to say that we should ask our horse if it is okay to get on their back. It is a temptation that I think we should yield to with great commitment. Yet we should perhaps be aware that the answer is ultimately going to depend upon our interpretation. Ultimately, it is the human who mounts the horse's back and not the horse that mounts the human on their back. Put another way, the question of to ride or not to ride has nothing to do with the horse but the human and, as such, the answer is ultimately our responsibility.

Is it not about a four-letter word?
But there was more. Michael Bevilacqua wrote something which left me feeling puzzled enough to chew on and chomp over for several days:

> I made a tacky, home-made video to go along with my book that was like a "special features" video along with movies. In it, I did say that, sometimes, *trying to explain this to people was like trying to explain how to love*. [Emphasis added.]

I looked at this and kept asking myself the question, "'Trying to explain *this*': What is *this*? What does he mean when he refers to *this*. Then I had an epiphany and the light came on. What has Michael Bevilacqua been trying to explain to people? Not only have I read his book several times and his articles too but I have also attended one of his seminars. *This* must refer to everything that he has been trying to explain in his publications and public events. And what was he trying to explain? How to love!

The real question

Trite? No. Profound? Absolutely! There are so many humans looking for a dream horse and a beautiful relationship with that product of their dreams. How? This is what we ask. How can we develop a beautiful relationship with our dream horse? In his book, appropriately entitled *Beyond the Dream Horse*, Michael Bevilacqua provides the answer, just as he has been doing in all of his work with horses and humans. Love. Simply love your horse! It is the beginning of everything.

Which led me to re-examine the question: To ride or not to ride? For far too long we humans have subconsciously been basing our entire relationship with horses on this question and the answer we almost inevitably come up with: ride. We have reduced our relationship with our so-called equine friends to the interface of the horse's back and the human's bum and almost all we do in relation to the horse is mediated by that interface. Perhaps it is time to replace the question, *To ride or not to ride?* with something else. Perhaps we need to move away from back and bum to horse and human. Is not the real question simply, "Do I love my horse?" and, if it is and my reply is "Yes!", then should I not simply go and love my horse and let all that we do together, horse and human, follow from that love?

Tales of love

Alexia's pen is poignant:

> Once one's eyes are opened they can never be closed again in ignorance and it seems doors have shut to some of what I thought were "simple" joys.

Ah, but have they shut? And if some have, have not others opened? I do not believe that I or anyone else can dictate whether a human should ride a horse or not. I do believe, however, that riding may be possible in my relationship with Pip. Yet the story that I wish to write with Pip is not of riding but of love and, if she allows me on her back, it will follow from that love.

IT'S ABOUT THE HORSE, ISN'T IT?

Can you recall the last time you were involved in a heated discussion about horses? Do you remember how insistent and emphatic you became, perhaps impatient or even incensed? You were so focused and intent on making your point, were you not? Perhaps your eyes were flashing, your hands clenched and your lips trembling. And just maybe even now you may shake your head and wonder how on earth the other person could not see and understand the simple logic of what you were trying to say at the time. Can you recollect what the topic was? It must have been important and, if it was, the chances are that it was one of those issues concerning horses which seem to erect barriers even between humans who share a deep, sincere commitment to their well-being. So what are some of these issues and are they really about the horse?

There was a time, as I recall, when the question as to whether the English or western style of riding was superior to the other was a source of heated debate. Fortunately, we humans have become more tolerant of different riding styles and the debate has moved on to more pertinent issues, such as those pertaining to the well-being of the horse, in particular, those raised through the emergence of the "natural horsemanship" movement.

Natural or conventional horsemanship

Perhaps the most defining contrast which has instilled itself in our perception of the relationship between horses and humans over the past few decades and how the latter should keep and care for the former is to be found in the gauntlet which "natural horsemanship" has thrown down to conventional attitudes towards horse husbandry and human-horse recreational pursuits and sports. Around the world humans have rejected and are increasingly rejecting the cynical use and abuse of horses, opting for what they believe is a more humane approach to our equine friends and more often than not referring to it as "natural horsemanship".

Presumably, it is the "natural" aspect which has captured our imagination, for it seems to embody an approach which is more commensurate with the nature of the horse, as we understand it. The outcome has been a growing movement of humans who are seriously questioning and challenging the assumptions and presumptions that underpin the hallowed bastions of the global horse establishment, and which have passed for equestrian truth for far too long, ranging from how horses are kept to how they should be trained and ridden. It is perhaps worth our while to dwell on some of the issues that have been raised in the process and whether they are indeed being resolved in the horse's favour.

Accommodation and care

Conventional horse care wisdom, especially as embodied amongst its leading proponents in prominent equestrian countries, such as England, the Netherlands, Germany, the United States and others, dictates that horses must be stabled separately and, if they are turned out, that this occur either individually or in small selected groups in tiny to small yards or fields often without shelter of any kind. Horses are usually rugged while they are turned out and in many cases while stabled as well during the cooler months. Frequently, the rugging is excessive. Invariably, the horses are also shod with metal studs euphemistically dubbed "horseshoes", a bit like calling a spade a shovel.

The "natural horsemanship" approach to equine accommodation and care, or at least its more advanced practitioners, have rightly challenged conventional practices such as those just mentioned, if for no other reason than that they are alien to the "natural" condition of the horse and as such must certainly be detrimental to the species. The logical follow-on must therefore be the pursuit of practices which are "natural" to the horse. Because wild horses live in herds outdoors, it is felt that a similar setup should always be used for horses in captivity allowing them to live in large fields. Similarly, horses should not be rugged and neither should they have to wear shoes. Rugless and barefoot is fast becoming the new standard amongst the more advanced proponents of a "natural horsemanship" approach to horse care.

The upshot is that there is an ongoing debate between the respective proponents of conventional and "natural" horsemanship as to whether horses should be kept indoors or outdoors, in a herd or on their own and be fitted with metal studs or not. Indeed, the debate between barefoot and shod can be particularly uncompromising if not downright vicious at times.

Riding

The art of horse riding has not been spared either. Whether of the English, western or even the Spanish variety, the proponents of conventional equestrian pursuits have not been and are still not reluctant to employ harsh instruments of domination and control, especially at the very summit of their respective disciplines. Featuring leather, buckles and even chains, bridles are often tight and oppressive enough to merit comparison with human sadomasochistic paraphernalia, as are the heavy, highly leveraged bits that are secured in horses' sensitive mouths. Small wonder then that conventional equestrian tack has inspired an entire branch of BDSM fantasy enactment known as ponyplay (I kid you not).

Conversely, it is no small wonder that horse lovers around the world have sought alternatives and have been quick to embrace those offered by the "natural horsemanship" movement. Bits have been discarded and bridles have been traded in for bitless variants or, more commonly especially amongst Western riders, the rope halter. And the debate between the respective proponents of bitted and bitless riding can become as vociferous as that between the supporters of shod and barefoot hooves.

Yet matters are not quite so vividly black and white when it comes to saddles. Perhaps this is because the treed saddles which are so typical of the conventional equestrian tradition are potentially kind to the horse, if they are flocked and fitted properly, and riding

114

occurs sparingly. They lift the rider's weight off the vulnerable spinal vertebrae and distribute it evenly across the muscles on either side of the spinal column behind the shoulder and over the ribs, that part of the horse's back which is more capable of weight-bearing than any other. Espoused by a considerable section of the "natural horsemanship" movement, most treeless saddles unfortunately do not do the same, although their supporters could rightly argue in many cases that they not only facilitate close contact between horse and rider, which is indispensable if the human is to move in sync with their mount and thereby minimise the discomfort which their weight may cause, but also avoid the damage which muscular tissue can suffer if it is constantly rubbing against an uncompromisingly rigid surface. Nevertheless, such awareness has not done much to reduce the debate between the respective proponents of treed and treeless saddles.

Training

A similar trend is visible in relation to training. Conventional horse training (although "training of the human to control the horse" would be a more accurate description) largely relies on negative reinforcement in the form of pressure and release with the emphasis placed on the application of external violence or the threat of it, using all of the instruments of dominance and control mentioned above along with an arsenal of others whose descriptions would fill a book.

Although the "natural horsemanship" approach also employs negative reinforcement in the form of pressure and release (see the chapter entitled Yielding to Pressure: The Reality of the Myth for a discussion of the use of pressure and release in both conventional and "natural" horsemanship and how alien this approach is to the horse), it is ostensibly kinder and, as such, more horse-friendly. Indeed, its proponents argue that their methods are derived from the way in which horses communicate with each other and, as such, they are more "natural" and therefore must be more horse-friendly.

Doubts

If there is any single instrument of training espoused by the "natural horsemanship" movement which conventional equestrian training has embraced more fully as part of its armoury than any other, it must be the round pen, even though its roots are far more firmly entrenched in the history of equitation. How can this be? If the round pen, which plays such an important role in "natural horsemanship", is accepted so readily by conventional horsemanship, perhaps we need to question just how "natural" it is?

And so the doubts begin and we turn to other instruments and methods employed by "natural horsemanship" practitioners. What of the bitless rope halter? Is it really kinder than the tight, bitted bridle? Vicki and I used to use a rope halter but then we abandoned it in favour of a firm but gentle webbing halter. The one I use for Pip is lined with soft rubber and I fasten it quite snugly on her head, yet always trying as far as possible to do everything on a slack lead. Why? Because more often than not a rope halter is made of thin to thinnish, hard, rounded bits of rope which are capable of exerting a huge amount of pressure without much force being applied on the lead. And immediately underneath the noseband of the rope halter there is very thin, fragile bony structure known as the rostral process. A tug on the lead, even a relatively gentle one, can hurt the horse in this sensitive spot. Yet there is always a bit of slack in the noseband, which means that a fiercer tug on the lead will not merely exert more force on that fragile structure but will also amplify it when the slack tightens suddenly. And yes, that bony structure can break quite easily and cause as much pain as the harshest bit. "Natural" and "horse-friendly", did you say?

And what of that other indispensable tool of "natural horsemanship", the "carrot stick"? When I went through my Parelli period, the only carrot part I found was the colour. For the rest, it was a stick but not merely that. It had a rope whip attached and both could be used to good measure to instil "respect" in the horse. I have always wondered why that tool is not called a "whip stick" or perhaps even "slapstick". "Natural" and "horse-friendly", did you say? (For a more extensive discussion of the "natural" of "natural horsemanship" see the chapter entitled *From "Natural Horsemanship" to Holistic Horse-Humanship*).

Doing "natural"

And so I could go on questioning the sincerity of "natural horsemanship", an approach which Klaus Ferdinand Hempfling dismisses as an attempt to secure the horse's "complete spiritual/mental submission" (*The Horse Seeks Me*, p. 58). Yet I must confess that "natural horsemanship" played a hugely important role in my path to the horse, for it marked the first time that I could stand in their presence without fear. Of course, I still needed to cover a great deal of distance down that path before I knew that I could abandon the round pen, the carrot stick and the rope halter and still feel absolutely safe with our horses. But this does not diminish the assistance which "natural horsemanship" provided me with on that path.

No, there is a more insidious side to "natural horsemanship" but it is not unique to it. Here I am referring to a huge temptation we humans regularly succumb to at the expense of the horse. It is our tendency to let our mind dominate our presence with our equine friends. In this case we look at what is supposed to constitute a "natural" approach to horses and then go about drawing conclusions which we apply to every horse. And so we insist that all horses must be kept in a herd out in the field all of the time, that they must be barefoot, that they must not be rugged, that they…. The list goes on. The idea of "natural horsemanship" becomes more important than the horses this movement was designed to serve.

Let us take a few examples. "Horses should always be kept in a herd outdoors." Really? What of horses that are kept in an environment where temperatures can reach 45°C (113°F), where constant rain turns pasture into mud, where they suffer sweet itch, where they are constantly attacked by horse flies during the day or….

"Horses should never be shod." Really. I must confess that I find this a difficult one, because I have yet to experience a situation in which real horse shoes (the ones you put on and take off like shoes such as ours but which are often inexplicably referred to as "boots") cannot do a better job than metal studs. The problem is that such shoes cannot be left on all the time. For any horse owner who cannot see their horse every day, this is a major issue. The only alternative is some type of stud, either metal or synthetic.

And so the list goes on....

Not unique to "natural horsemanship"
Yet this predisposition to generalise for the purposes of creating a model and then to insist on compliance with it at the expense of the horse is not unique to "natural horsemanship". Very often we can see the same approach exhibited by some practitioners of even more "horse-friendly" approaches, for instance, those who espouse positive reinforcement training methods, such as clicker training. Because it works so well with some horses, we are all too ready to ignore the fact that it can create treat-focused monsters out of others, as we have seen with our own mare, Anaïs.

Then there are those horse owners and carers who have decided against riding ever again, prompted in part by their knowledge – backed up by scientific research – that riding can compromise a horse's health in as little time as the equivalent of a brief coffee break. Of course, this is commendable but should you generalise this approach to the extent that you interpret this as a prohibition of riding in all cases? What of the horse that requires extensive movement in order to remain healthy but whose health would be compromised by excessive movement on a circle, which is as much as one can expect from groundwork with the healthiest of humans in addition to their free movement in the herd? Are we to condemn that horse to relative inaction because it does not accord with our model of what is horse-friendly, namely, not riding?

Then there are others who have not only decided not to ride again but to "allow their horses to be horses again", essentially turning their properties into horse sanctuaries where their equine friends are at liberty to roam around together. Of course, this is well-intentioned but one could also legitimately question whether it actually helps those horses. After all, horses in the wild travel distances of up to 35 km (21.8 miles) a day, movement which is essential to their physical and mental well-being. How many of us have properties which are so large as to permit this type of movement without human intervention? And if we do intervene, what will we do?

About the horse, really?
And so we find ourselves with a horse wondering what to do to provide the creature with the type of accommodation, care and treatment which would best benefit their physical and mental well-being yet still be within our means. We draw on our knowledge and experience to identify and assess various alternatives. Perhaps we have developed guidelines which we may wish to employ in the course of our assessment and decision-making.

At the end of it all though, when we examine our decision in the cold light of day, can we really say that it is about the horse? Not just any horse but the creature before us? Can we truthfully say that the decision which we have taken is in the best interests of that particular horse? And is not this the only reliable litmus test? And if it is, perhaps we may also want to ask ourselves if it is really worth our while to become embroiled in debates about what is best for horses which leave us with eyes flashing, hands clenched and lips trembling, when really all that the horse before us requires is that we act in their best interests in the situation and at the time in which they find themself? Should you expect anything more of yourself? Would your horse if they were ever capable of considering the question?

LESSONS TAUGHT ME BY MY HORSE

Today I celebrate the fifth anniversary of one of the most special moments in my life, the day when my mare, Pip, formally entered into my life. And as I celebrate that moment and the joy which I have been privileged to experience with this horse, I reflect on some of the lessons that she has taught me and the immense gratitude I feel for daring to learn them. Because these lessons have so greatly enriched my life, I would like to share them with anyone who cares enough for their horse to dare to do the same.

Lesson 1. Be present, be calm and do nothing!

Liberty with a human may be a traumatic experience for a horse that has been denied the opportunity to live as one. This is the very first thing that Pip showed me. I had taken her into a large jumping arena, just the two of us, on our first day together. When I removed all of the tack, she was seized by an overriding panic which caused her to frantically rush up and down the fence line. No contact with her was possible and hence no communication.

Instinctively, I felt a need to halt her frenzy, to restore contact and to reassure her but without using any physical restraint on her body. Holding a rope in one hand and switching it to the other if required, I managed to confine Pip in a corner of the arena and then just stood there trying to relax while searching her eyes for contact. Eventually, it came and then we just stood there doing absolutely nothing for as long as it took for her to calm down. This was a ritual which we employed many times before it was no longer required.

Lesson 2. It is impossible to control a horse!

On the face of it, not too much effort is required to control a horse or even dominate them. You can use force or the threat of it. Alternatively, you might opt for bribery or trickery. You may even assign fancy names to these types of approaches, calling them positive or negative reinforcement, punishment, operant or classical conditioning, habituation or the like. Taking it further, you could even immerse yourself in detailed studies of the theories underlying these terms and attempt to apply them.

Pip was the epitome of a horse controlled by a human. She had been ridden to an advanced intermediate level of dressage in the Netherlands and was relatively easy to control, albeit that she had the reputation for being a fiery ride, prone to bolting with a novice. Indeed, I even found it so easy to dominate my mare, that I ended up doing so with embarrassing frequency, especially when she began to reveal to me the futility of my apparent success. She would do everything I required but would switch off while doing so. Responding to stimuli was possible but meaningful communication not. My initial response was frustration, anger and more domination: in a nutshell, impotence!

Yes, I could control the creature before me but was it still a horse? Pip had developed a capacity to do all that was required of her by consciously withdrawing from it and going on autopilot. She had become the robot that training was designed to create. Vicki and I used to travel around the world to attend the World Equestrian Games and the equestrian events at the Olympic Games. What I saw there was a more refined version of what was essentially the same. What I have since seen achieved with positive reinforcement is much kinder but in the case of trained behaviour, the outcome is essentially the same: the creature is controlled but the horse – that sensitive, sentient, graceful, inquisitive and powerful being – has gone AWOL, absent without leave.

Lesson 3. Expect nothing!

This has been one of the most difficult lessons. Down the years I had been taught that the object of interaction with a horse was to demand instant obedience in the manner that I required, and that this was the purpose of all training, an approach which fit the bossy part of my nature like a glove. Not much has changed since then, albeit that demanding and cajoling are now referred to as "asking" but perhaps I am yielding to cynicism.

One of the most testing times of this lesson is when you enter the field which serves as your horse's home and you hope that now will be the day when your horse comes to you of their own accord without being trained to do so. You may have to fetch your horse after all. Worse still, you may even have to try and catch the creature, because they resist all of your efforts to be nice and appealing.

Why not just expect nothing? After all, you have nothing to lose. So you try this ... day after day ... and nothing happens ... until ... one day the magic happens. And the more you learn not to expect anything, the more your horse gives you. Yesterday Pip did not come immediately. She was dozing in her current band of three mares and four geldings. I joined them and we shared a very special, peaceful moment: being there, doing nothing ... until ... Pip was ready to come with me and Anaïs followed just as Vicki arrived.

Lesson 4. Trust is the strongest bond between horse and human!
Often when we refer to trust in relation to horses, we treat it as a one-way street from the human to the horse. How often have we not heard that the horse needs to learn to trust the human? Part of the truth, as Pip has taught me, is that a horse does not need to learn to trust. They either trust or they do not.

Similarly, Pip has helped convince me of a lesson that Anaïs and our geldings, Farinelli and Gulliver, had already taught me. It is this. Trust is a two-way street. You either trust your horse or you do not. I remember early on in my relationship with Pip there were times when she swung her head around and, if I was in the way, I got bashed. At a certain point she started to take pains to avoid bashing me. Now, if I happen to be in the way, she lifts her head over mine. The experience is similar to those I have had with Anaïs and our geldings.

Trusting your horse can also be a truly liberating experience. About a year ago I rode Pip out on the trail solo for the first time. I did so after only having ridden about five times in seventeen years. And I did so with nothing but a bitless bridle and a bareback pad without any stirrups, the first time that I have ever done so in my entire life. A little short of 59 years of age at the time, I simply had to trust my horse in a situation like that or stay off her back. She did not let me down either literally or figuratively. The feeling was awesome.

Lesson 5. Be reliable, dependable, a source of security and trust yourself!

This is a lesson which goes hand-in-hand with expecting nothing. When Pip came to me, her experience of humans had been dictated by their demands and expectations of her. Instead of being allowed to live like a horse, she was confined to a stable with the exception of a few hours a day and her behaviour was dictated by force or the threat of force with the aid of equipment which would not be out of place in some despot's torture chamber.

Over time Pip came to realise that, not only am I not a threat to her and actually a fun person to be with, but also a human who helps her live like a horse, who rushes to her assistance whenever she comes down with an injury or ailment, and who provides her with care and security. More importantly though, Pip has shown me that, if I trust myself to the extent that I no longer need to try and prove myself with her, I am a human who is trustworthy.

Lesson 6. Be a friend to your horse!

Ultimately, the type of relationship which has worked best with Pip is that of friendship. Being a friend to her is a lesson that, once learned, she has reciprocated. But what does being a friend mean? At the end of the day, it boils down to a simple four-letter word, one which I had difficulty acknowledging in my relationship with Pip until I met Michael Bevilacqua. It is this: love.

The love of a friend is that which empathises and empowers rather than claims and denies. I take delight in all that enables her to enjoy her life as a horse. There are times when we stand apart and there are times when either or both of us seek contact with each other. Ultimately, there is no need to insist on boundaries.

Lesson 7. One size does not fit all!

There was a time when I was a "natural horsemanship" proselyte. You know the type, generally a human who insists that no horse should be kept in a stable, that they should always be kept outside in a herd without metal studs on their feet or rugs on their backs, that they should be ridden bitless, that they may only wear rope halters, and that they should be driven from behind rather than pulled from the front.

By being so different from our other horses in as much as they are so different from each other, Pip has confirmed that horses, like humans, are individuals. As such, the "solutions" that they require are bespoke, tailored to each one's needs. I have seen too many horses suffer at the hands of zealots, no matter how well-intentioned they may be. Let us celebrate the individuality of our horses.

Lesson 8. Horses are holistic creatures requiring holistic solutions.

From the day on which she entered my life, Pip has impressed upon me the need to find holistic solutions for her requirements, much as our other horses have also done. Addressing her lopsided forequarters reflected in unbalanced shoulders and uneven feet has required a combination of ongoing movement in a herd, appropriate hoof trimming, straightness training and bodywork. Similarly, the treatment of her blown tendon demanded a combination of confinement, technologically facilitated monitoring, red-light treatment, bodywork and regulated activities. In these and all other cases, there was no single silver bullet.

Lesson 9. Helping horses can help humans!

For years I have looked on "equine-aided", "equine-facilitated" and "equine-guided" activities with some misgivings. In the main this is probably because these terms impute a role to the horse which is secondary to that of the human. They also seem to suggest that it is acceptable for us humans to unload our emotional or psychological baggage onto horses. In particular, I have grave doubts about the use (I use the term advisedly) of horses in programmes designed to boost the profitability of private companies and, as such, increase the earnings of a privileged few at the expense of the many.

In my limited experience there are very few horses and humans, if any, who come to each other as creatures who have not been traumatised to some or other degree. The interaction of the two species with each other has the potential to benefit both. Examining my own situation, I must confess that I have truly benefited from my interaction with our horses, in general, and Pip, in particular. They have fundamentally changed my outlook on and approach to life.

Yet they have done so, not through any "equine-aided", "equine-facilitated" or "equine-guided" activities but rather through one specific type. Quite simply, it is through helping horses that they have helped me. Not only was the latter not expected, it was not even sought. Perhaps it is through such commitment and intent that horses can truly help us become....

Lesson 10. Become the kind of human a horse seeks to be with!
When all is said and done, I truly believe that this is the litmus test of a human's ability to be fully human with their horse. And it is simultaneously the lesson that encompasses all of the others. If all of us could do this with our horses, how much more fulfilling would their lives not be?

HORSES AND THE MYTH OF LEADERSHIP

"You have a leadership problem with your horse. Your horse does not recognise you as a leader." Your trainer may have said this to you on occasion or something similar to it. As a result, you may have shrunk into your shell and seized the first opportunity to slink off quietly to find a quiet corner in which to lick your wounds or rap yourself on the knuckles for failing to be a leader to your horse. But what does this mean, "being a leader to your horse"? Does it really mean what they tell us? That your horse needs to respect you and do what you want them to do? More importantly perhaps, we may want to ask ourselves if there is any sense in the concept of leadership in relation to horses and, if there is, to what extent, if any, it is meaningful and useful in our interaction with our equine friends. After all, if the concept of leadership in relation to horses serves no purpose, why use it?

"Leadership" and its rationale

Within the domain of interaction between horses in captivity and humans the term, "leadership", and its derivatives ("leader", "to lead" and so forth) are usually employed by "natural horsemanship" practitioners or trainers who seek to identify with a "natural" approach to horsemanship. The concept is said to have its roots in studies of the natural interaction of horses with each other in the wild.

In its simplest form, the rationale advanced in support of the concept of "leadership" within equine communities is premised on the assumption that horses in the wild live in a homogenous herd. Such a herd, the rationale continues, is led by a single horse, who is recognised as "the leader" by all of the other horses in the herd.

This is where the rationale diverges depending on the stream within the "natural horsemanship" movement. The most simplistic rationale contends that the leader of the herd is an "alpha" horse, one that demands and receives acknowledgement of their "leadership" capabilities from their peers. This is the "psychology" underlying Parelli's "Seven Games", which – the official Parelli website argues – "establish a language between horse and human that enables clarity of communication and positions you in the alpha role – head of the herd, even if there's only two in your 'herd'" (http://www.parelli.com/the-seven-games.html – without the hyphen – consulted on 7 June 2017).

The notion of an "alpha" horse positioning themself as the "leader" of the herd also underlies the "join-up" approach adopted by Monty Roberts. According to the official Monty Roberts website, the fundamental question which a "trainer" asks the horse when employing his method is this: "Will you pay me the respect due to a herd leader and join and follow me?" And this question is asked after the "trainer", working in a round pen … begins Join-Up® by making large movements and noise as a predator would and begins driving the horse to run away", which is ultimately typical "alpha" horse behaviour (http://www.montyroberts.com/ab_about_monty/ju_about/ – consulted on 7 June 2017).

Some streams within the "natural horsemanship" movement are uncomfortable with this simplistic approach and have accordingly developed somewhat more nuanced versions of the overall "rationale" for introducing the concept of "leadership" into the horse-human relationship. One such nuanced version is that presented by Marijke de Jong, the founder of "Straightness Training", who, although not a typical proponent of "natural horsemanship", has borrowed heavily from it in this respect. She has devised a fairly elaborate rationale in support of the concept of "leadership" (see http://straightnesstraining.com/the-rider/horsemanship/be-the-leader-with-your-horse/ – without the second hyphen – consulted on 7 June 2017). In her model an equine leader is "calm, stable and wise", such as an old mare but definitely not a stallion, because his "role is to keep the herd together and to keep intruders and predators away from the herd'. The stallion, as she sees it, is the "group coordinator". Yet she is a bit ambivalent, because she maintains that, "Leadership involves choosing the direction for the group and providing security to all others in their herd," a description which in part covers the role she ascribes to the stallion. And it is precisely this ambivalence which De Jong subsequently holds up as the model of leadership which we humans should subscribe to in our dealings with our horses:

> You can help your frustrated and confused horse return to a balanced state by being a good leader! As humans we should copy the great qualities of the "leading mare" and the "group coordinator" and see them as our role model!

How natural are the "natural horsemanship" leadership rationales?

If the rapidly growing influence of "natural horsemanship" is anything to go by, it is difficult not to conclude that the "natural horsemanship" leadership rationales represent a seductive narrative. Ascribing one of the most crucial tenets of "natural horsemanship", namely "leadership", to equine nature in the wild clearly holds great appeal to those of us who are actively seeking an alternative to conventional horsemanship with its emphasis on force or the threat of it, and who are increasingly turning back to nature in search of authenticity. Yet how natural are these rationales?

Equine ethologists, such as Lucy Rees and Victor Ros, have conducted extensive studies of herds of "wild" horses in Europe and still do so. Their findings are also corroborated by the observations of "wild" horse documentary makers, such as Ginger Kathrens, the cinematographer behind the legendary *Cloud* series, and reveal the following aspects, which largely debunk the claim that "natural horsemanship" rationales for leadership have their basis in nature:

• in the wild there is no such thing as a homogenous herd of horses led by a single or even several horses. Rather, depending on its size, a herd is made up of several or numerous bands of horses, each of which is usually controlled by a single dominant stallion;

- although there is a pecking order within each band, it is not permanent. On the contrary, it varies constantly depending on the circumstances and makeup of the band;
- no single horse within a band constantly and consistently takes the lead in guiding the band to safety or resources such as water and forage;
- the role played by the stallion is not merely to safeguard the security of the band but is predominantly geared towards maintaining and extending his equine assets, and this may occur at the cost of some of the horses comprising those assets.

Although it may be possible to produce more examples, we would do well to bear in mind that the herds of horses whose study constitutes the basis for the "natural horsemanship" narrative of leadership are not naturally wild but feral and, as such, we have no way of gauging the impact which captivity has had on those herds in the long term.

But perhaps the single most telling reason why the "natural horsemanship" leadership rationales are anything but natural lies in the fact that the horses with whom the "natural horsemanship" approach is pursued live in an absolutely unnatural environment, namely, captivity and the ramifications of this are so utterly fundamental as to completely negate the "natural horsemanship" approach. The chief differences responsible for this are as follows:
- horses in captivity generally do not live in a herd;
- where they do live in a "herd", the horses comprising it may not form bands, which is often the case if the herd is too small or the space to which they are confined is too limited;
- the membership of the herd depends on the arbitrary selection of horses by humans, with the result that no organic development occurs as in the wild;
- in captivity up to half or more of the herd may consist of utterly unnatural horses. Here I am of course referring to geldings, which simply do not occur in the wild and it goes without saying that the nature of a stallion is completely changed by gelding

them. This is after all the reason why humans mutilate (castrate) them;

- as such, the development of largely harem bands around a controlling stallion usually does not occur;
- similarly, there is little evidence of the emergence of "lead" mares in captivity;
- what we do see in captivity and generally not in the wild is the emergence of "dominating" – so-called "alpha" – horses, which, as Marijke de Jong points out, is probably due to human influence rather than anything else.

"Leadership" practices in "natural horsemanship" training

By this stage it may be tempting to conclude that, if the "natural horsemanship" leadership rationales have no basis in fact, there should be no need to consider the "leadership" practices employed in "natural horsemanship" training. If we were to do this, however, we might risk throwing out the baby with the bathwater. After all, it is at least remotely conceivable that perhaps one or more of such "leadership" practices may have some basis in the way that "equine leaders" deal with other horses in the wild.

So what would constitute "leadership practices" within the "natural horsemanship" approach? Here is a list that I have produced on the basis of my observations of "natural horsemanship" in action:

1. "join-up";
2. aggressive behaviour and physical force;
3. driving;
4. psychological squeezing.

1. "Join-up"

Introduced by Monty Roberts as the basis for his approach to "natural horsemanship" training, "join-up" is perhaps the most controversial of these "leadership" practices. Let us examine what it is based on a description provided by Monty Roberts, himself:

> Working in a round pen, one begins Join-Up® by making large movements and noise as a predator would and begins driving

the horse to run away. She then gives the horse the option to flee or Join-Up®. Through body language, the trainer will ask, "Will you pay me the respect due to a herd leader and join and follow me?" The horse will respond with predictable herd behaviour: by locking an ear on her, then by licking and chewing and dropping his head in a display of trust. The exchange concludes with the trainer adopting passive body language, turning her back on the horse and without eye contact, invites him to come close. Join-Up occurs when the animal willingly chooses to be with the human and walks toward her accepting her leadership and protection. This process of communication through behaviour and body language and mutual concern and respect, can be a valuable tool to strengthen all other work with horses.

According to Roberts, "The result is a willing partnership in which the horse's performance can flourish to its full potential, rather than exist within the boundaries of obedience" (http://www.monty-roberts.com/ab_about_monty/ju_about/ – without the hyphen – consulted on 7 June 2017). For a moment let us suspend our disbelief at the notion that it is possible for a "willing partnership" to develop between horse and human which is based on the human "making large movements and noise as a predator would ... driving the horse to run away". In order to assess whether "join-up does indeed produce a willing partnership, it is important to understand precisely what is involved. Put another way, does the description of "join-up provided by Monty Roberts actually tally with his characterisation of it. First of all, we are told, the trainer drives the horse "to run away". Is this true? Absolutely not. After all, this is taking place in a round pen. As such, the trainer is driving the horse along a fence-line which never ends and, horses being as smart as they are, pretty soon the creature learns that there is no end in sight to the movement which they are required to endure. So how would you expect a horse to respond to a situation of hardship (being driven) to which there appears to be no end? You would not be wrong if you were to conclude that you would expect them to give up, because ultimately that is the only alternative provided to the horse.

So what does the horse do? They lock an ear on the trainer, lick and chew, drop their head and then walk towards the trainer. This, we are told, is "predictable herd behaviour". Really? Recall the beginning of Monty Roberts' description for a moment: "one begins … by making large movements and noise as a predator would". Now we are asked to believe that a horse is not going to respond to the movements and noise of a predator with the type of behaviour that is characteristic of a herd's initial response to a predator (flight or fight, in the first instance). So why does the horse not flee as it normally would in nature? Well, quite simply, the horse *is* fleeing from the predator as far away from the threat as possible along the perimeter of the never-ending fence-line but they are prevented from fleeing far away by that very same fence. So why does the horse not stand and fight? Possibly because join-up usually never occurs with a stallion or, if it does, not without the human holding a whip in their hand while chasing the horse.

Instead of flight or fight, the horse locks their ear on the trainer? Why? Is it not because this is a typical response to anything threatening which is chasing them, namely, they need to be aware of the origin of the threat? Licking and chewing usually denotes some form of relaxation on the part of the horse following heightened activity or stress. In this case do the licking and chewing not suggest an awareness on the part of the horse that, although they are being chased, they will not be attacked? And when the horse drops their head and walks to the trainer, does this not suggest resignation to the inevitable rather than an embrace of the situation as a willing partner? And when the horse "chooses to be with the human and walks toward her", is this behaviour really an expression of a willingness on their part to be with the human and to accept the latter's leadership, as Roberts claims? Or is it not more tellingly, the first significant expression of learned helplessness on the part of the horse? After all, if the only choice available to the horse is to continue racing down an endless fence-line or to move away from it towards the centre, where else are they going to go but towards the centre? And just guess who coincidentally happens to be standing in the centre. Join up or give up?

2. Aggressive behaviour and physical force

You are already aware that Monty Roberts' join-up is based on human predatory behaviour. This he candidly admits himself. In this case though we are not talking about just any form of human predatory behaviour. More specifically, join-up relies on the form that is most threatening to the horse: the chase. Much of this type of predatory behaviour can still be seen in what passes for the "natural horsemanship" version of "liberty work".

Taking their cue from a horse that puts their ears back and accompanies this signal with hard eyes and firm lips to elicit specific behaviour from a subordinate in the pecking order, following up that show of force with a lunge and bared teeth and more if it is not forthcoming (so-called "alpha" behaviour), "natural horsemanship" practitioners frequently also adopt an aggressive posture when training a horse to move away from them (including yielding their hindquarters), which is on most occasions. Pat Parelli's instructions for "playing" the first part of the "yoyo game" (the fourth of the seven games comprising Level 1, the aim of the first part being to get the horse to move backwards in a straight line) illustrate the point. This version was published in *Natural Horse Magazine* (see http://naturalhorse.com/archive/volume3/Issue7/article_8.php?cmtx_ sort=4, consulted on 23 June 2017).

After assuming a position in front of your horse with your 12-foot lead rope attached to your horse's rope halter at one end, the other firmly grasped in your sweaty hand about an arm's length from your horse's nose, you are now advised to, "Give your horse a *Schwiegermutter* (German for mother-in-law!) look like you are another horse laying his ears back". In a horse this may be all that is required in order to elicit the preferred behaviour because of all the energy informing that signal. Energy, however, is not what "natural horsemanship" deals in, which is why the *Schwiegermutter* is not enough and the human is then advised to resort to a mechanical device to elicit the desired behaviour from the horse. And just what is that device?

Well, it is the lead rope but it is just not going to be used for leading but for more aggressive purposes. While looking at your horse as the stereotype of a fierce German mother-in-law would, you are advised to lift your hand and wiggle your index finger at them. If everything remains at the mechanical level only, you may rest assured that your horse will stand exactly where he is and perhaps look at you quizzically. This means that you will probably need to move to the next level ("up the ante" is what Parelli calls this), which is to gently wiggle the lead rope sideways while still playing German mother-in-law with your eyes, the idea being that the moment your horse takes the smallest step backwards, you will stop glaring and wiggling at them. So what happens to the lead rope when you do this. The gentle wiggle created by your hand advances up the rope until it impacts against the halter and ruffles the jaw. If your horse still does not take a step backwards, you go up another level and increase the vigour of your wiggle. And as you do, notice how the lead rope amplifies the wiggle to create a wave which crashes against the horse's jaw, especially if the lead rope is connected to the rope halter with a large metal connector, as is usually the case. By now your horse should seriously be beginning to consider a step backwards if they have not already done this. And if they have not, just up the ante and hope your horse can handle the metal slapping against their jaw.

By now there is probably no need to connect the dots. You get the picture, don't you?

3. Driving

Driving refers to the process of compelling a horse to move in a particular direction by exerting pressure on them to do so, using motions which may include physical force but which normally imply the threat of force, usually without touching the animal and more often than not in a forward direction, although it may be in a backward direction, as in the case of the first part of the yo-yo game.

As such, it is more an expression of psychological compulsion than anything else. It is a technique which is most successful when coupled with psychological squeezing. The trigger for the exertion of such pressure may be refined to a subtle signal which goes a long way to creating the semblance of a spontaneously willing equine partner.

Driving is perhaps the only "leadership" practice which "natural horsemanship" has sourced from the wild. This is what a stallion resorts to in their efforts to keep their band safe and secure for their pleasure. In the wild this is also to a large extent effective in keeping the horses comprising the band safe from predators and other dangers.

In its most cynical form, driving in a "natural horsemanship" context is coupled with leading on a loose lead. Because the lead droops in a lazy loop from the human's hand, it gives the appearance that no force or threat of force is employed. The lead is said to have a smile in it. Yet the only way the horse may be induced to move, is by driving them using the other hand. And no, there is definitely no smile in the drive!

4. Psychological squeezing

This is a term that I have coined to refer to what I personally feel is one of the most diabolical and unscrupulous forms of horse training ever devised. Essentially, psychological squeezing employs the driving technique coupled with intense psychological pressure designed to render every alternative form of behaviour other than that demanded of the horse so unpleasant that the horse will exhibit the form of behaviour required of them by their human "trainer" for no other reason than that every other available alternative has been rendered so unacceptable that the behaviour demanded of them becomes the only acceptable way forward. In this sense the required behaviour is squeezed from the horse very much as paste is squeezed from a tube through its opening.

As such, the technique of psychological squeezing is nothing more nor less than psychological manipulation designed to achieve human domination of the horse without the use of physical force. Because this technique is both exceedingly effective and simultaneously creates the illusion of compliance by a willing equine partner, it is also extremely enticing to the human who seeks to have such an illusion become their reality in their dealings with horses.

Psychological squeezing can be used in a variety of situations. It is also quite effective in not so subtly teaching your horse to load themself into a trailer. Simply ensure that the only attractive place to be is in front of the trailer and advancing into it, all other alternatives having been rendered unacceptable to the horse. In the saddle, I have seen this technique used to induce a horse to go forward. Simply spend some time bending the horse into the tiniest circle possible at the walk and, if possible, advance on to tiny figure-eights. Within a few minutes your horse will probably welcome the opportunity to walk forward briskly in a relatively straight line.

"Leadership" tools
Have you ever stopped to consider the tools that "natural horsemanship" practitioners rely on in their efforts to convince the horse that they should become a "willing" partner to the human while simultaneously accepting the latter's "leadership"? Here I am referring to the rope halter, lead rope, "carrot" stick and in many cases also the round pen. At first glance these tools appear to be a far friendlier alternative to the conventional equestrian establishment's reliance on tight-fitting bridles with their bit (or bits if you're planning on competing at the most senior levels of the dressage hierarchy) and drop nosebands, not to mention the ubiquitous whips of all sizes and spurs. I know I had a warm, fuzzy feeling when I embraced these "leadership" tools during my relatively brief foray into Parelli's version of "natural horsemanship", convinced at the time that they and his approach were more horse-friendly.

Then I started learning more about the nature of the horse and I re-examined these tools of "leadership". Let us start with the "carrot stick", which is actually more stick than carrot. Indeed, the only similarity with a carrot in the case of the Parelli variant of such a stick is the colour. To all intents and purposes, a "carrot stick" is nothing more than a strong, relatively long rigid stick, capable of inflicting more injury on a horse than most whips, with a long cord attached to enable it to be used as a whip as well, giving the human two tools of control for the price of one. It is generally used in the pursuit of the "natural horsemanship" version of leadership to drive the horse outside of one's bubble, to drive the animal backwards, to drive and control the hindquarters and to drive the horse in mindless circles around the human to demonstrate the latter's "leadership".

Then there is the rope halter. If ever there was sign that someone had "progressed" from conventional to "natural" horsemanship, then this must be it. Gone is the ultra-tight bridle and webbing "head collar" (a misnomer if ever there was one, a "collar" being by definition something which goes around the neck) in favour of the loose, "horse-friendly" rope halter. Indeed, the "natural horsemanship" practitioners even use it as the preferred head gear when riding. So is it really "horse-friendly"? Pick up one and examine it. Note the rope. It is usually quite thin, hard and round. Imagine what it would feel like if it were suddenly drawn tight against your skin on part of your body where there is little more than skin covering bone. Note also that, when the rope halter is placed on a horse's head, there is a good deal of slack and, when you note this, consider also what the effect could be when the slack is suddenly tightened. Knot the rope halter as you would when putting it on a horse making sure that you have a lead rope attached to it appropriately, place the poll end over your shoulder and stretch your arm out until you can just loosely drape the "noseband" over the back of your fingers. It feels quite comfortable, does it not? Now imagine that you are riding or leading your horse, your shoulder to your fingers being their head. Suddenly a kangaroo leaps out of nowhere (I speak from experience) and you instinctively clutch the lead rope as your horse takes off like a rocket in any direction other than the one in which you were heading. As you imagine this, clutch the lead rope attached to the halter around your arm and pull it down hard and fast enough to give yourself some idea of what half a tonne of horse feels like when it moves in a different direction from you and your lead rope. Does the rope halter bite? And where does it do so? Right there: the equivalent of the poll of the horse with its collection of sensitive tissue and their equally sensitive nose, just about where the nasal bone thins to a very vulnerable wafer. Surprised? You should not be. This is what the rope halter is designed to do in an effort to secure "respect" for the human's "leadership". Now consider that this exercise presupposes the occurrence of an accident. What if the rope halter were also to be used as an effective means of control during training, as when driving the horse to the end of the lead rope until their rope halter digs in and forces them into a circle?

Well, surely if the lead rope is used without pulling or driving the horse into their rope halter, that should not hurt the creature, should it? This is where the "natural horsemanship" model's reliance on driving to secure "leadership" comes into play again. Have you seen a "natural horsemanship" practitioner drive a horse with a lead rope? When this occurs at liberty, a small part of the lead rope is swung around the hand either in the direction of the horse or obliquely. Either way, if the horse does not yield to the swinging rope it will be whacked on whichever protuberance remains in the way, usually the rump or the nose. When the lead rope is attached to the horse through the rope halter, it is frequently used to drive the horse backwards. The human does this by swinging their end of the rope horizontally which creates waves in the rope that amplify as the zigzag in the rope heads towards the horses jaw just behind the mouth. For added persuasion of the human's "leadership" qualities, the lead rope is usually attached to the rope halter with a relatively large, heavy metal connector and, when it connects with the horse's jaw, as it often does, the horse is usually instantly convinced of the human's "leadership" powers.

And so on to the round pen. Surely this tool cannot be as effective in persuading the horse to accede to the human's "leadership"? Consider the fence of the round pen from the horse's perspective. Where does it end? And when the horse is driven around the perimeter as they usually are, is the end ever in sight? And so we come full circle to Monty Roberts. Is it really join-up or is it not give-up, the horse giving up all control over their own movement, their body and their spirit? And if it is, where does this lead? Learned helplessness?

Reinforcement and driving

If you have ever trained with a "natural horsemanship" trainer, you will probably have noticed that they avoid the use of treats as rewards or any similar form of positive reinforcement. Indeed, more often than not they will pride themselves on eschewing treats. Instead of treats or other positive reinforcement rewards, they insist that the horse show the human respect and yield to the latter's "leadership". But is it really the human's "leadership" which the horse is required to accede to or is it something else.

The "leadership techniques" employed by "natural horsemanship" rely to a limited extent on pressure and release. This is a negative reinforcement training technique which entails the application of physical pressure to a horse's body to induce them to exhibit a certain form of behaviour and which is released when that behaviour is exhibited by way of a "reward". Although this technique is utterly alien to a horse (see the chapter entitled *Yielding to Pressure: The Reality of the Myth*), it is also employed extensively in modern conventional equestrian pursuits.

Within the "natural horsemanship" paradigm, the pressure and release technique acquires more sinister overtones as a practice which is predominantly designed to obtain the horse's recognition of the human's "leadership", often under the guise of an inspiring rationale replete with references to "respect", "willing partnership" and the like. The Parelli method employs this technique both extensively and ruthlessly as a precursor to the preferred "leadership" practice of driving, especially in the course of the euphemistically termed "Seven Games". An initial failed attempt at driving the horse to play such a "game" with the help of a so-called "carrot stick" is followed by instructions to "up the ante" with rising levels of physical force and aggressive energy.

Repeated often enough, the logic goes, the horse will learn to avoid the physical force and aggressive energy to yield to the initial attempt to drive them in a particular direction. Very soon then the horse will learn to respond to the human's attempt to drive them immediately. The illusion of a willing partner responding to a slight request on the part of the human will then become a reality.

Leadership or domination

So far, human domination has largely been implied at most rather than explicitly mentioned in this discussion of horses and "leadership" with one exception, namely, "join-up". At this point it is probably opportune to deal with it explicitly. In order to do so effectively, we need to agree on terminology which is specific to this subject matter. Accordingly, I propose to employ the following terms bearing the meanings assigned to them below.

"Dominate", "dominating" and "domination" are terms which I use to describe the process involving a human successfully exploiting their power over a horse to control them usually by employing force or the threat of force. "Dominance" and "dominant" are terms which are unfortunately more ambivalent. This is because both of these terms may be used with entirely different meanings. They may be employed to denote such domination. For instance, "dominance" may be employed to refer to the process of domination while "dominant" may denote its outcome. Yet both of these terms may also bear a more neutral meaning in the sense of being higher up the pecking order, as it were. For instance, a human carer has a dominant position in relation to their horse in that the human controls the conditions of their horse's accommodation, feed, care and training, amongst other things. This places the human in a position of "dominance" in relation to the horse to that extent. It is usually the context which reveals the meaning of a particular use of the terms, "dominance" and "dominant". Unfortunately, the context may not always be clear.

Based on the definitions employed here, it should be clear by now that the human "leadership" practices described above are little more than techniques designed to make it possible for a human to dominate and control a horse. Similarly, the "leadership" rationales outlined above are no more than a sophisticated justification for humans to dominate and control horses. Or are there alternative explanations which I (and many others) just fail to see?

Yet is it so cut and dried? Take the "natural horsemanship" trainer, Buck Brannaman. Touted as the "Zen Master" of the horse world, Brannaman is admired as a man who has shown himself to be calm and in tune with horses, so much so that he has even become the subject of a popular documentary film. The "horsemanship" is indeed inspiring by many if not most humans' standards. Yet, when I watch the videos, really look at the horse and ask myself just where is the creature in all of this and just how willing a partner they are, I am left with questions? And you?

Deception on a massive scale?

In that the "leadership" rationales serve to legitimise human domination of horses and the use of techniques designed to achieve such domination, the question arises as to whether their employment and that of the terms used by those employing them to denote the techniques and tools of domination which they employ do not represent a widespread con job, wilful deception on a massive scale.

Of course, such deception would only exist if it could be shown that it was accompanied by the intention to deceive. This would entail passing judgment on fellow humans. It is my experience that such judgment helps neither horses nor humans and, as such, is a futile exercise. What would be more beneficial, I suspect, is to find ways of relating to horses which benefit both them and their carers.

Caveat

At the risk of shooting myself in my foot, as it were, I must confess that I have seen a tiny number of "natural horsemanship" practitioners manage to develop a fairly close relationship with their horse in spite of the techniques and tools that they use. They appear to have a close bond with their horse and are able to communicate with them rather than rely on conditioned behaviour or learned helplessness.

What these exceptional [I use the term advisedly here] "natural horsemanship" practitioners seem to have in common is, first and foremost, a profound commitment to the well-being of the horse. Secondly, this is coupled with a sensitivity to what the horse is communicating through both energy and signals and an ability to feel into what is happening between them and their horse. Thirdly, and as importantly, such humans tend to be content and the energy they radiate is that of quiet joy. Perhaps Buck Brannaman is also just such an exceptional "natural horsemanship" practitioner.

Leadership

By now we have reached the stage where we may legitimately ask whether any concept of leadership does or should play a role in the relationship between horses and humans. Marijke de Jong contends that, if a human fails to show leadership in relation to their horse, the latter will do so and that this will inevitably result in a dysfunctional equine, one that may even become aggressive and dangerous. Perhaps this is true, although it could be difficult to prove as there are so many things that humans do or fail to do which create traumatised horses.

Drawing on his martial arts (Aikido) experience, the energetical interaction which it involves and the self-assurance which it confers, Mark Rashid, has become a champion of "lightness" in horse training. He has also advanced the concept of "passive leadership" (see http://www.markrashid.com/docs/leadership.pdf, consulted on 7 June 2017). This is how he explains it:

> There are two types of leaders in a herd situation. The alpha, or lead horse, that rules by dominance, and passive leaders that lead by example. The passive leaders are usually chosen by other members of the herd and are followed willingly, while alphas use force to declare their place in the herd. Passive leaders are usually older horses somewhere in the middle of

the herd's pecking order. They are quiet and consistent in their day-to-day behaviour and don't appear to have much ambition to move up the "alpha" ladder. As a result, there appears to be no reason for them to use force to continually declare their position in the herd.

Alphas, on the other hand, are usually pretty far from being quiet and consistent in their behaviour. They are often very pushy, sometimes going as far as using unprovoked attacks on subordinates for the simple reason of declaring their dominance. As a result of this behaviour, the majority of the horses in the herd will actually avoid all contact with the alpha throughout the day.

By this stage we may have concluded that, if the herd actually avoids all contact with an "alpha" horse, then such a horse simply cannot be a leader, the implication being that horses only have a single type of leader, a passive one, according to Rashid's approach. So what makes a "passive leader"? Here is Rashid's answer:

Passive leaders have "earned" that particular title with the other horses by showing them they can be dependable in their passive behaviour from one day to the next. In other words, they lead by example, not by force.

Yet assuming that Rashid is right and that this is the way that horses regulate issues of "leadership", and also assuming that they have any, does this mean that we humans should try and emulate horses in our dealings with them. I do not know about your horses but ours are pretty smart. They have worked out a long time ago that I am not a horse. Indeed, whenever I have tried to emulate a horse in my dealings with them in the past, they have been less than impressed. So if this is not the answer, what is?

Friendship

As Chuck Mintzlaff of "Friendship Training" fame has known and preached for a long time, by far the closest bond one horse has with another or even any other is that of friendship. Take a horse's friend away from them and they will bellow in pain, abandon their food and pace, if not run, the fence line. Although Mintzlaff has used this close bond as the basis for his Friendship Training programme, I tend to agree with Michael Bevilacqua that "friendship and understanding have nothing to do with training". You simply cannot train friendship! The flip side of this coin is that you can most certainly fake friendship with a horse through training.

The basis of any true friendship is a four-letter word: love. If there is anything that I would describe as the most profound truth about the relationship between horses and humans that I have ever learned from the horses, this would have to be it. As humans, we have the potential to be the greatest friend a horse could ever have, not because of what the horse can give to us but rather what we can give to the horse without ever expecting anything in return.

This is not a clingy, cuddly friendship that I am referring to here, although there will be times when a horse will want to do just that with their human friend. Rather, I am referring to the type of friendship in which the horse views the human as a friend who has no need to prove themself, who is content, solid, dependable, reliable, caring and trustworthy, who is the human they seem to be, who is capable of feeling and communicating with them, who does and shares nice things with them, who is empathetic and empowering, and who is all of this without ever asking anything in return. This is the basis of everything: friendship. For it is then that the horses give everything of their own accord and acknowledge their human friend.

So is this too tall an order for a human? When I look around me and see how much time, energy and money humans devote to trying to take the same or slightly different shortcuts with horses for five, ten, fifteen, twenty years or more and still feel frustrated in their dealings with horses, then I have to confess that friendship has turned out to be a far better option. It has been ten years since my light-bulb moment while watching Klaus Ferdinand Hempfling together with his equine friend, Janosch, in the wild. I suspected it then but I know it now: friendship is the basis for everything and anything that we wish to do with horses which is genuine and authentic.

FROM NATURAL HORSEMANSHIP TO HOLISTIC HORSE-HUMANSHIP

As I survey the situation prevailing in the world of the domestic horse in countries which boast some of the largest populations of this category of equines, mainly in Europe, the Americas and the Antipodes, it seems to me that, with the exception of the racing industry and those sectors in which horses are used as beasts of burden for the purposes of generating a source of income for their owners, the conventional approach to keeping and training horses in captivity is under threat from a wave of apparent reform which in many instances is proving to be more harmful to the species than the abuse which it claims to abolish. Here I am referring to the phenomenon of "natural horsemanship", which originated in North America through the influence of people, such as Ray Hunt and the Dorrance brothers (Tom and Bill), was made famous by the likes of Monty Roberts and Pat Parelli, and achieved international respectability through the awards heaped on the film, *Buck*, which documents the influence of the "natural horsemanship" practitioner, Dan M. "Buck" Brannaman, who served as the model for Nicholas Evans' book, *The Horse Whisperer*, and the film of the same name, starring Robert Redford as the "horse whisperer", Tom Booker. So what is this phenomenon called "natural horsemanship", why do I think that why do I think that its approach is harmful and is there an alternative?

Benefits of "natural horsemanship" husbandry

In the past few years Vicki and I have made a point of looking for so-called "natural" or "natural horsemanship" livery yards for our mares. Generally speaking, they are establishments in which horses are kept barefoot without rugs and in a "herd", with ample outdoor space and indoor cover to enable them to move and interact with other horses whenever they choose to do so while obtaining relief from the elements when necessary. Some also choose to adopt a more horse-friendly health-care regime, eschewing the use of potentially harmful practices, such as conventional vaccinations and worming products, and avoiding the excessive use of antibiotics. Most of those that we have come across are Parelli-inspired outfits where a version of his approach is practised (or something similar). We have opted for such livery yards, not because we feel that they are perfect but because they enable horses to live more closely in line with their intrinsic nature than conventional livery yards.

By contrast, conventional horse husbandry denies the intrinsic nature of the horse and seems to be hell-bent on creating an array of problems that require expert, expensive and often invasive intervention. Breeding programmes create monsters, some of whom are so enormous that they can barely support their own weight, much less a rider as well. Premature weaning and an upbringing in the absence of socialisation produce psychologically unstable equines, a situation which is exacerbated by the introduction of a training regime long before the horse is capable of undergoing it without suffering more mental trauma, not to mention the physical conditions created as a result. It takes a strong horse to survive the obstacle course that is their early upbringing and the few available are snapped up by professional trainers, leaving the mentally traumatised and/or physically impaired equines for lesser mortals such as you and I. In conventional yards horses are generally kept in stables for up to 24 hours a day and, if they are turned out, this usually occurs in small fields with only a few fellow equines and then only for part of the day. More often than not they are also kept with metal studs (also known as "horseshoes") nailed to their hooves and are ridden with the aid of metal and leather restraints and instruments of force, such as bits, spurs, martingales and the like. Any interaction between horses and humans is usually confined to riding or training perceived to be a prerequisite for that bum-back relationship. It is fair to conclude that such conditions are not in the interests of the horse's physical, mental and emotional well-being.

Dangers of "natural horsemanship" training

In his book, *It is Not I Who Seek the Horse: The Horse Seeks Me*, Klaus Ferdinand Hempfling convincingly argues that the "natural horsemanship" approach is designed to persuade the horse that the trainer's pressure is more attractive than all of the other options available to them. It is for this reason, and this alone, that the horse ultimately yields to the trainer's will and produces the behaviour which the trainer requires of it. This is the underlying premise of Monty Roberts' "join-up".

In this sense one might also add that such an approach produces a refined version of learned helplessness. In a nutshell, a horse is said to suffer from learned helplessness if they surrender and give up all resistance, because it has become clear to them that all avenues of escape have been closed off. The refinement of the "natural horsemanship" variant of learned helplessness lies in the fact that one of the avenues of escape that has been closed off is nevertheless preferable to all of the others.

Where it simply relies on psychological repression secured through brute physical force or the threat of it, some variants of "natural horsemanship" are less refined. The result is ultimately and almost inevitably learned helplessness, the few exceptions proving the rule. It is only in this manner that one can secure the horse's cooperation in charging blindly on a circle at the end of a longeing lead while their human consults the latest post on their "natural horsemanship" page on Facebook.

Perhaps the most insidious danger of "natural horsemanship" lies in its name. It is insidious in that its name is misleading and self-deluding. It is misleading in that it masks the harm caused by the perpetrator. And it is self-deluding in that the name suggests to the human pursuing the "natural horsemanship" approach that they are helping their horse, whereas there may be a good chance of them doing so in relation to the care and accommodation of their equine friend but almost none at all when it comes to interaction between the two species. Having said that, I have been privileged to witness the utterly liberating work of a Level 2 Parelli instructor who frequently manages to create magic with horses, albeit in spite of and not because of the "natural horsemanship" approach which she pursues. Her secret? Awareness, intent and the joy of life.

Differences and similarities

Overall, as I have indicated, there are a great deal of differences between "natural horsemanship" and conventional horse husbandry. Those differences pertain primarily to care, accommodation and horse-human interaction. Yet there are also similarities. What both approaches tend to have in common is, firstly, that their supporters generally feel that their approach is superior to any other. All too often they even do so to the extent that they feel quite justified in vilifying any approach which does not correspond to theirs.

Secondly, both conventional and "natural" horsemanship rely on yielding to pressure, an approach which is founded on a fundamental misunderstanding of how horses deal with pressure, as I have shown in the chapter entitled *Yielding to Pressure: The Reality of the Myth*. While many "natural horsemanship" practitioners are keen to point out that they ride bitless, those who rely on harsh rope halters forget that such devices can inflict as much harm (if not more) on a horse – through their nose and poll – than a bit in their mouth. Something similar may be said about the heavy snap at the end of a lead rope and the way it is waved towards and even against the horse's jaw to get them to move backwards, producing a creature at the end of the lead who is confused and terrified.

Thirdly, the "success" of both approaches relies to a large extent on conditioned behaviour and, where that fails, brute force or the threat of such force and ultimately even learned helplessness on the part of the horse.

Fourthly, to some or other extent both conventional and "natural" horsemanship seek to desensitise the horse to any stimulus which is deemed to pose a danger to the human on top or in the vicinity of the creature. Yet it is precisely that sensitivity that horses require if they are to be alert to anything which might endanger them or their human carer and if communication between horse and human is to occur clearly but gently.

Fifthly, through their apparent but illusional "success" both approaches entice horse owners and carers to resort to them as a means to achieve personal gain in the form of wealth, status or self-aggrandisement.

Sixthly, as in the case of all favoured models, there is a temptation on the part of the practitioner of either the conventional or the "natural horsemanship" approach to adhere to their preferred model at the horse's expense. An example in the case of "natural horsemanship" may be found in many of its practitioners' insistence that a horse not be rugged even if this means that the creature suffers sweet itch and scrapes their skin open in a desperate attempt to find relief. Similarly, there are those who insist that horses not be stabled under any circumstances unless they are sick or injured, with the result that the animal may be exposed to intense heat and sunlight, not to mention pests, in hot climates instead of being stabled during the day and turned out at night where this is the only possible alternative. Another example may be found in some "natural horsemanship" practitioners' refusal to make the transition from hoof studs to barefoot in stages (hind feet first and front feet later) or with the temporary aid of shoes (what is commonly referred to as horse "boots", a bit like calling a spade a "shovel").

Beyond natural
Then there is the concept of "natural" itself. "Natural", the word does sound so utterly sexy, does it not, especially to those of us who increasingly insist on finding a way of keeping and interacting with horses, which prioritises their interests and well-being? It is enticing in its presumed promise of serenity and balance, is it not? This is how horses survive in the wild. This is how they relate to each other in the absence of humans. This "natural" condition, it should be our guiding principle, our beacon to light our way through the dark

spread by conventional husbandry and horsemanship. All that we do with horses should fit within this paradigm, should it not?

But are we not fooling ourselves? Is nature always nice? And where, I ask you, do horses survive anywhere on this planet in the absence of human control or influence? Even the feral brumbies of Western Australia and the world's only true wild horses, the Przewalski of Mongolia – amongst the most sparsely populated parts of the earth – are unable to escape it. And are these wild and feral horses no more than a small fraction of the globe's equines, the vast majority of whom simply try to survive under the rigours of human domination, which range from firm to savage. Is it not time to admit that, when it comes to horses, "natural" is a myth, something which largely exists within our imagination as a romantic illusion and not much anywhere else?

Romantic illusions

Is it not time to jettison our romantic illusions of what is "natural"? Yet, what if there is more? If you strip away "4 Horses Creek", "Equinatural" or any other name we humans may bestow on an equine establishment to nurture the notion of "natural", and if you then coldly examine all that is done in its name (and not merely the "aberrations" which I mention above), how much will you find that is utterly "unnatural"? You will certainly not need me to help you answer that question and you will definitely not need me to come up with the answer: "a lot". Which is not to suggest that, because it is "unnatural", it must therefore be harmful to the horse. Yet we are left with a very awkward question and it is this: if much (or perhaps even most) of what is done in the name of "natural" horse-keeping and horsemanship is "unnatural", are we not missing the point which is at the heart of both, namely, the horse? Which in turn leads to another curly query and it is this: if the pursuit of things "natural" is missing the point, could it not be harmful to the horse?

Let me illustrate this with an example. In the pursuit of all that is "natural" in relationship to horses, many of us are unequivocal in our demand for them to be allowed to live in a herd with ample resources rather than be stabled for up to twelve hours or more every day. Yet there are times of the year in some parts of the world, where doing so is akin to condemning them to profound suffering because of flies and horse flies, in particular. Yet prevention is easy. Simply confine the horse to a dark indoor area and the flies disappear as though a magician had waved a wand. It would not be "natural" to do so, surely? But would it not be more "unnatural" not to? Or do the questions simply represent a dangerous red herring, because neither is in the interests of the horse. But if they are not, what is?

Back to the horse
Fortunately, there would appear to be a very simple solution to this dark riddle and perhaps the brumbies can help point the way. Australia is a vast country and it is home to some 300,000 brumbies. They may be found in areas that vary greatly in terms of their geography and climate and include the arid Outback, subtropical coastal areas, high country of Snowy River fame, and even parts of the Monsoon-inundated tropics. Yes, human intervention occurs and it is often cruel.

Yet even without it the life of a brumby is harsh. Apart from the challenges peculiar to the geography and climate of the areas in which they find themselves, Australia is a country that is hard, particularly on a species such as the horse, which is innately alien to it. If the drought does not bring a horse down, perhaps a cyclone will. But then again, it could be one of the many species of amongst the world's most poisonous snakes to which the country is home, or perhaps a "saltie", one of the huge, prehistoric salt-water crocodiles that inhabit the rivers and billabongs of the tropical north. Alternatively, the brumbies may find it impossible to compete with both indigenous and introduced species for feed and water, amongst them hundreds of thousands to millions (depending on the species) of feral camels, buffalo, donkeys, goats and the like. Nature can be and often is cruel. No humans are required for this.

Perhaps we need to abandon our preoccupation with trying to ensure that all we do for the horse is "natural". And perhaps we will find it easier to do this once we realise that nature can be and often is harmful to the horse. Put another way, "natural" is not by definition in the horse's interests, assuming that the condition still exists on a planet which is already suffering greatly from the "unnatural" intervention of humans and is forecast to suffer even more. In fact, "natural" can be harmful to the horse to the point of claiming its life. If she could speak, my mare, Pip, could confirm that "natural" can burn fear into her soul as effectively as any bit, spurs or whip may have done in her former life.

Perhaps it is time for us to abandon the concept of "natural" when we search for appropriate ways of caring for and interacting with our equine friends. Perhaps this is the moment when we should refocus on the very point which inspired the ideas of "natural horse-keeping" and "natural horsemanship. And perhaps it is now that we should return to that very point: the horse. If we are truly committed to the well-being of the horse, then surely the measure of all we do for and with our equine friends must not be whether it is "natural" but rather that it is in their interests. Perhaps we should now leave "natural" for what it is and go back to the horse.

Holistic horse-humanship
This is not to deny that "natural horsemanship" has not served any positive purpose. In my own development it marked the first time that I felt entirely safe with horses. This was an essential first step towards what I have since experienced with horses. Nevertheless, it seems to me that the "natural horsemanship" approach has reached its use-by-date for the reasons outlined above.

Now is the time not merely for a new approach but an entirely fresh paradigm, one which appears to be developing organically amongst people around the world who are committed to becoming and being the kind of human a horse seeks to be with. This new paradigm, which I have come to call "Triple H" (HHH) to denote holistic horse-humanship, appears to be based on the following principles:

- it assumes that it is the human who needs to change and not the horse, and that this change entails that the human regains their humanity;
- it is designed to improve the horse's well-being;
- it is holistic in its scope and remedies;
- it is experiential in that learning and development occur through experience and reflection on it;
- except in unusual circumstances, the horse's evident happiness is the key determiner of the satisfactory nature of its accommodation, care and interaction with humans;
- however, this does not excuse us from our own responsibility to ensure that the horse is not misused or abused, especially where the horse may seem to indicate that they are content but we ourselves are aware that the situation is simply not good enough;
- the term "human" is used not only to include all genders but also to emphasise the need for a humane approach.

Being a Triple H solution

And so I go in search of a holistic horse-humanship solution for our mares in Spain and our geldings in Australia. Although life does not come with guarantees, the beauty of such a search is that it has already found the genesis of such a solution. It begins in me, in you and in all of us and to a greater or lesser extent we can be that solution wherever we encounter horses, whatever the conditions with which they have to contend. All we need is awareness, intent and the joy of life. The rest will take care of itself!

HORSES AND THE ART OF FOLLOWERSHIP

So when you walk into the field that your horse knows as home, do they come to you unasked? Perhaps they come to you when you call? And does your horse then walk freely with you to the gate? So if your horse chooses not to come to you, does this say something about your leadership (or lack of it)? Or does it say more about your horse's desire to follow you (or lack of it)? But does not the one imply the other, that by definition a leader has a follower? Perhaps. Yet should your horse choose to follow you, does that not make you your horse's leader? Really? Or is there perhaps something more to following than simply a passive acceptance of "leadership"? Could it be that horses have mastered the art of followership and that it is also through and because of this that we have so much to learn from them?

Leaders or followers?

Of course, these questions in turn seem to beg the question as to whether horses are leaders or followers, or at any rate whether any horses assume the role of a leader at any particular circumstances in their day-to-day life. The mythology of "leadership" which is so inherent in the "natural horsemanship" movement (see the chapter entitled, _Horses and the Myth of Leadership_, for more detail) makes mention of at least three types of "leadership" which are said to occur amongst horses in the wild and may therefore serve as roles which we humans could assume in order to become a leader to our horse. First, there is the "alpha" horse, then there is the "lead" mare and finally there is the stallion.

Let us start with the stallion first, if only because there is a temptation amongst humans to consider a stallion to be a natural "leader" given his nature, status in the herd, especially as the head of a predominantly female band of horses. Within the same breed, stallions generally tend to be bigger and stronger than their female counterparts. A stallion utilises his size and strength to capture a harem band of mares – usually accompanied by foals and young stallions – more frequently than not after a fight with the existing band stallion, although a band may be left on its own if its stallion has a fatal encounter with nature. As the young stallions grow and develop an interest in sex, there comes a time when the band stallion banishes them from the band (at about two years of age) and they generally join a group of bachelor stallions and remain with them until such time as they manage to take over their own band of mares and young.

You may have seen videos of band stallions in the wild "snaking" members of the band to ensure that they remain together. This you may be tempted to view as an example of leadership. To the extent that a stallion does this in order to protect his band against whatever he deems to be an external threat, this could indeed be interpreted as a form of leadership, for it does offer its members safety and security and this may be the reason why most, if not all, of the mares in a band remain loyal to their stallion. However, we need to be aware that the primary reason why the stallion does this is to safeguard what he views as his legitimate assets. It is this rather than any desire to be a leader which motivates the stallion. In addition, during the frequent times that the stallion strays from his band to chase off predators or perceived arrivals, there is ample opportunity for any of his mares to wander off. Although few *choose* to do so, there is at least one documented case that I am aware of in which a mare does exactly that. In *Cloud's Legacy: The Wild Stallion Returns*, the second in the *Cloud* series of videos, filmmaker Ginger Kathrens introduces us to a very pregnant roan mare whom she calls Blue Sue. Cloud captures her from his brother, Red Raven. Months later the mare retires from Cloud's band to foal but does not return. Shortly afterwards we see Blue Sue reunited with Red Raven, a newborn foal at their feet. Whether the mares remain with their stallion or not is ultimately their choice irrespective of the fact that the majority *choose* to do so. And it is precisely this element of choice coupled with the stallion's preoccupation with safeguarding his equine assets that suggests that the mares' "followership" is far more significant than any "leadership" on the part of the stallion.

A so-called "alpha" horse is said to be one that makes their presence emphatically known within a herd by resorting to dominant behaviour directed at fellow herd members, usually in order to secure some sort of advantage for themself at the expense of the latter. Many horse people have dispensed with this notion, arguing convincingly that most, if not all, of the members of the herd usually avoid such dominant horses for the simple reason that they do not want to be on the receiving end of their aggression. There are even some commentators who suggest that such "alpha" horses are actually an aberration created through human abuse, as they are not normally found in the wild. We may therefore dispense with the "alpha" horse as a role model for "leadership".

As an alternative to the notion of an "alpha" horse being a convincing leader, Mark Rashid postulates the occurrence of "passive leadership", being a form of leadership by example on the part of a middle-ranking, older mare in the herd. There is fairly well-documented evidence to suggest that an established mare within a band usually takes the lead in moving towards a watering hole, a meadow in which to graze or something else which is of benefit to the group. However, it would appear that this role is not reserved for any specific mare. Rather, it may vary from one occasion to the next with different mares *taking the lead* (as opposed to "leading") in different circumstances. In addition, it is important to realise that the mare does not turn around to draw the attention of the other members of her band and gather them around her to move off in a particular direction. Rather than consciously leading, she is simply the first to move in a particular direction. The rest of the band, including the stallion, who usually takes up his position at the rear of the group, may *choose* to follow or not. So again we have choice playing a major role but in relation to following and not leading.

However much choice they have in deciding whom to follow, what is abundantly clear from the above is that horses *prefer* to follow rather than seek to lead. And the reasons why they prefer to follow are dealt with below.

Pecking order

So what about pecking order in a herd: is this not a form of leadership? Interestingly enough, with the exception of the band stallion, who may claim priority within his group and is usually accorded it if he does, the so-called pecking order is something which is usually only seen when horses need to compete for resources. If sufficient resources are available for the number of horses making up a band in the space available to them, there is no need for the members of that band to compete with each other. The other side of the coin is that, where few resources are available relative to the size of the group and the space available to them, or only just enough, there is usually competition and some type of pecking order becomes apparent.

It should therefore come as no surprise that observers of horses in the wild note little in the form of a pecking order within the bands that they observe, as there are normally ample resources available in the area in which the horses roam. Rather, it would appear that a pecking order is typical of horses kept in captivity. And where a pecking order is apparent, it has nothing to do with leadership but everything to do with gaining access to resources and, because competition is involved, it is usually accompanied by aggression. The Welsh ethologist, Lucy Rees, who has spent many years observing and studying feral horses in Spain, amongst other places, notes that there is likely to be twenty times more aggression amongst horses in captivity than in the wild (Epona.TV: https://epona.tv/-bonding-behaviour-largely-ignored-by-scientists – without the first hyphen – consulted 20 July 2017).

An ideal concept of leadership

If you were to ask a fairly enlightened human to provide you with the definition of a "leader", you may be presented with something of this nature: a leader is someone who is capable of exhibiting empathy, who is trustworthy and empowering, who sets an example, who is charismatic, and who inspires, motivates, encourages, and ultimately liberates. Let us assume for a moment that you actually manage to become someone who fits this description. Would this make you a leader? And if it does, would you not have followers? After all, you can only be a leader by definition if someone follows you, surely?

But what if no one knows that you are this kind of person? What if no one has heard about you, that you are capable of being all of these things? You would not have any followers, would you? Which means you would not be a leader by definition even if you do have all of these qualities, surely? And is this not in turn another way of saying that, even if you possess all of these qualities, which would make you probably the most enlightened "leader" the world has ever seen, would you not ultimately depend on someone first learning about you and then, based on that knowledge, *choosing* to follow you before you can become such a leader?

So, if having these qualities would not necessarily make you a leader, what would they make you? A friend perhaps? And your horse, would they *choose* to follow you if they experienced all of these qualities in you?

Reasons to follow

The chances are that your horse would not choose to follow you, even if you possessed all of the qualities that would make you the most enlightened leader the world has ever seen. Why not? To answer this question we need to examine why horses choose to follow others of their own species.

Essentially, there are two main reasons why one horse will choose to follow another. One of these is friendship but not as an enlightened human might care to define it. Truly, it is far more basic. It is feeling. It is bonding through the gut. Unfortunately, our awareness of friendship amongst horses is largely based on our observations of domestic rather than wild or feral horses. As Lucy Rees has noted, ethological studies have largely focused on agonistic (conflict-related) behaviour amongst wild horses rather than affiliative (companionship-related) conduct (see Epona.TV: https://epona.tv/bonding-behaviour-largely-ignored-by-scientists – consulted 20 July 2017). There are some things which science cannot explain and friendship is one of them. Essentially, as I experience it with horses and my best friend and partner, friendship is an energetical and emotional confluence of two life forces, which can become more important to the creatures involved than even food. Indeed, they will even risk safety and security to be with each other. So too with horses.

Then there is that special form of friendship which also involves a sexual relationship. As I write this, we are three weeks down the track from a reunion between our mares, Pip and Anaïs, on the one hand, and Pingo, a gelding who was castrated late and still behaves like a stallion right down to recruiting his own harem band within a herd of a little under forty horses within 24 hours, the only time I have ever seen anything like this occur amongst domesticated horses (see my blog post entitled *Nature, Riding and the Bottom Line* at http://horsesandhumans.com/blog/2016/06/04/nature-riding-and-the-bottom-line/ for more details). Although Pip and Anaïs have been close friends for years now, Pip is in season and she constantly leaves her female companion to go in search of her male lover. While the relationship between Pip and Pingo is largely sexual at present, there is a great deal of tenderness and caring in the way they interact with each other. Amongst other forms of endearment, they brush their muzzles against various parts of each other's body, spend time standing close together even to the point of touching, rest the underside of their heads on each other's necks and gently rub up and down each other's mane. From time to time Anaïs tries to intervene between the two of them. She literally moves between them, faces Pingo and paws the ground. Initially, I thought she was doing this in order to protect Pip but later on I noticed that she herself had come into season and was clearly demanding attention. A little astounded and nonplussed at first, Pingo would ultimately have none of that. He had set his heart on Pip and Anaïs simply had to go. So he chased her away and she withdrew smartly, looking very subdued. Within twenty-four hours Anaïs was no longer in season, yet she again tried to intervene between the lovers (since then I have also noticed another female member of the band do the same and she too was not in season at the time and subsequently discovered research amongst feral horses reveals that stronger mares actively discourage breeding between their stallion and weaker mares in the band). Now Anaïs remains in the lovers' vicinity marking her time until the two female friends together return to being the core of Pingo's harem band after Pip comes out of season.

Secondly, there is a collection of reasons why one horse will *choose* to follow another and they have everything to do with equine well-being. Here I am referring to those which serve to help the horse feel safe, secure and content. Horses *choose* to follow other horses to escape danger, find food and water and enjoy each other's company in natural surroundings, and so forth. In other words, any kind of movement which a trusted horse makes in a direction which makes sense to other senior members of the band is likely to result in them *choosing* to follow that horse with the foals, adolescents and the stallion taking up the rear.

Choosing to follow

There are several conclusions which we can draw from our observations of horses choosing to follow other horses, especially in a captive herd. They may be summarised as follows:

- horses choose whether to follow another horse or not;
- horses choose which horse to follow;
- horses can exercise this choice as and when the occasion arises;
- similarly, horses can choose not to follow another horse, whenever they want to;
- horses are more likely to follow a friend (and even more so one with whom they have a sexual relationship) or a trusted horse whose movements are known to be in the interests of their well-being;

161

- following does not imply the existence of a leader;
- as such followership is a more appropriate model for understanding equine interaction than leadership.

There is a temptation to view following and followership as passive activities. However, because choice plays such a crucial role in determining whether a horse will follow another of this species or not and because such choice is so fully in line with horses' active commitment towards sustaining and preserving the communal nature of their social structure, we need to view following and followership as what they really are, namely, active undertakings with a hidden power which even borders on the subversive.

The power of followership
The flip side of choosing to follow may be found in a choice not to do so. The decision of the roan mare, Blue Sue, to abandon Cloud and return to the father of her foal, Red Raven, is a particularly moving example of this. Nevertheless, such an occurrence is quite rare. The most profound example of the power of followership amongst horses may be found in their choice not to follow a bully. The vast majority of horses actively deny the power of "leadership" to a so-called "alpha" creature who throws their weight around and seeks to dominate others of the species. Let us not underestimate this power of choice. Conversely, it is also within a horse's power to choose to associate with such a dominant horse at times. An example of this was when Pip returned to the herd in Belgium after recovering from her tendon injury. Duke was around to greet her and Pip responded warmly.

To illustrate the potential of this power, let us try and imagine an equivalent in human society. In our so-called free Western democracies, we humans get to exercise the type of choice that horses take for granted every single day only once every three to seven years depending on the country we live in. This we do in the form of elections. Our choice of whom to follow is limited by strict rules governing the nature of political parties. Yet it is effectively limited far more by the media, which is largely held and controlled by vested private interests or corporations that effectively have little or no form of public accountability. And once we have exercised our choice, we are denied every right to withhold followership from whomever assumes power. Most Western democracies deny ordinary people the right to hold referendums on important matters between elections and, if they do, the outcome is not binding on the "leadership" of the day. More importantly, there are no nation states that effectively allow ordinary people to revoke their support and recall the government to pave the way for a new exercise of choice. Indeed, there are countless measures to enforce our compliance with whatever our "chosen" leaders decide to foist on us, from the economic in the form of the threat of unemployment to the criminal if we decline to have up to one third or more of our hard-earned income spent on implementing policies which we do not support in the name of tax. In practice, our form of so-called leadership seems to have more to do with the pursuit of vested interests by a small wealthy minority with the connivance of politicians driven by self-interest who ultimately rely on manipulation, control and force or the threat of force to "lead" us under the guise of "democracy" and the "rule of law". As a result, the disparity between the obscene wealth of a few and the diminishing disposable income of the many has become so acute that some organisations, which have traditionally served as the guardians of this societal imbalance are warning against the inherently destabilising contradictions which this disparity represents. And I have not even got to the less developed parts of the world.

Now imagine our human society with all its warts and pimples being run according to the principles of followership which guide communities of horses. Gone would be the bullies, those who rely on subterfuge, manipulation and on incessant streams of exhortations to materialism coupled with dumbed down media entertainment, the modern equivalent of gladiatorial games, contests to dominate and control us and, ultimately, legalised violence or the threat of it in the name of justice. No longer would the tail wag the dog. The notion is utterly subversive and, dare I say it, liberating. Perhaps we need to reassess our idea of followership as opposed to leadership?

When you next go to your horse
So when you next open the gate and enter the field which your horse knows as home and watch your horse approach you, should you not perhaps stand in awe and feel blessed to know that your equine friend has *chosen* to come to you and that they are doing so, not because they have been trained (conditioned), cajoled or threatened into doing so. Rather, does your horse not recognise in you a human they seek to be with: a friend and being trusted with their well-being?

THE POWER OF BEING WITH HORSES

Have you ever experienced it? You and your horse are walking side-by-side. It may be on a forest path, a hill track, anywhere. Your horse's breath is raspy and warm against your forearm in the cool of the morning, comforting almost. You relax into an even stride. The four-beat rhythm of the hooves scuffing the dirt next to you hold your attention. You try and identify each foot as it hits the ground. It occurs to you that the rhythm of your stride is beginning to match that of your horse. And then it does. A bird calls in the distance. You smile. Why not quicken the pace? You thrust the base of your pelvis forward slightly and feel the energy course through your loins. Your horse responds. Now let us try to slow down. So you drop your energy and your equine friend slows as well. But what if you were to run? You feel the energy build up in your body as you prepare to do so. And suddenly your horse breaks into a trot well ahead of you. You almost halt in amazement but instinctively follow in a celebration of the power of shared being.

Being

So what is this "being" of which I speak? And what power can it confer on you and anyone else who cares to embrace if? You are a human being. So am I. But what does this mean? Perhaps more importantly though, what could it mean if you or I were truly intent on living in full the life of a human being?

Here "human" is used to identify our species and to distinguish it from others. But what about "being"? It is a grammatical form which has the linguistic function of a thing, what grammar would call a noun, yet its structure is derived from a verb (an "action word"), namely "be", but not just any form of it. "Being" is the form which we associate with the present continuous, a grammatical structure which denotes an ongoing action, such as "living", "beating" and "breathing". And it is in this notion of ongoing action that we can begin to discover the secret of "being".

Motion

Stop for a moment and consider yourself. You are sitting still, doing nothing. Motionless, you may think you are but you are not, not if you are alive. Every single part of you is in motion, however minutely it may occur. Your heart is pumping, your blood is flowing, your lungs are bellowing, your cells are replenishing, and so the list goes on. Everything within you is in motion, even those parts of you which you may be tempted to feel are not, such as your bones. It is only the speed of that motion which varies.

Look around you. Perhaps this constant motion is only inside you. After all, you are seated and, as such, you certainly cannot be moving around. Really? Consider for a moment just where you really are while busy being you. All around you there are signs of movement. For instance, as I write this I can hear voices of people coming and going accompanied by the sound of a car door closing followed by a gate opening. In the distance I spy clouds swirling over hazy mountains in the distance, while the tantalising smell of lunch cooking wafts in from the kitchen. Simultaneously a breeze tugs at my hair and caresses my skin. Pause for a moment and sense the movement around you as you take a break from reading this. What can you hear, see, smell, touch, taste? You are influenced by this motion and perhaps influence it in turn.

Now let me help you extend your awareness of your ostensibly fixed position. You find yourself in a particular location on our planet. Although it may seem as though you are not moving, the Earth is spinning around on its axis at an average speed of approximately 1,674.4 kph (1,040.4 mph), taking us with it and allowing us to experience day and night. Simultaneously, we are hurtling through space in a rotating orbit around the sun at a velocity of 107,200 kph (66,600 mph) to give us the seasons. And at the same time our planet's axis rotates at a tilt. As if that is not enough, our solar system, which we share with other planets, such as Mercury,

Venus, Mars, Saturn, Jupiter and Pluto, is part of a gravitating galaxy of stars, planets and other celestial phenomena – the Milky Way – which in turn gravitates with other galaxies, which in turn…. And this is where it gets mind-boggling.

Suffice it to say that from its tiniest to its most gigantic part, the universe's normal state is one of movement. In this sense the objective nature of "being", human or otherwise, is constant motion. It occurs before we exist as human beings, in the process of human conception, gestation, birth, life, death and decomposition, after we cease to exist, and both within and without our bodies while we exist. And where there is motion, there is energy.

Energy

Many humans have a tendency to feel very uncomfortable when presented with the concept of energy. They avert their face, cast a quizzical glance, raise their eyebrows or their eyes glaze over, as though they are having to contend with an interlocutor who has elected to dwell amongst the fairies. Yet energy has a sound scientific basis in Western society and acquired it during the twentieth century largely due to the work of a man to whom science owes much. By now you may realise that I am referring to Albert Einstein, he of the well-know equation, $E=mc^2$, where "E" stands for energy, "m" for mass and "c" for the speed of light.

What this equation implies is that every physical body which has mass also contains energy and that the smaller the body, the larger its energy content is likely to be relative to its mass. Expressed in layman's terms, this is a bit like saying, "Dynamite comes in small packages".

Although Einstein is widely misquoted and quotes are imputed to him for which there is no evidential basis, especially in the New Age press and in social media, his discoveries and theories have gone a long way towards helping Western science understand the universe of which we are part. As such, there is an objective scientific basis for the concept of energy and its existence in every single life form, including ours. Put another way, in that Einstein and others recognised the essential nature of energy in material phenomena, Western science finally came to acknowledge what has been the accepted wisdom of Chinese teachings for thousands of years. What it is yet to do is understand and explain the fundamental role played by energy in living creatures along with their interaction with each other, and the importance of learning how to interpret and control it.

Awareness

So why is energy so important? Quite simply, it is so because it is the key to communication between humans, and between us and other species, such as the horse. It is both the fuel which powers movement and resistance to it, and the medium through which we can sense or feel the energy coursing through ourselves as well as other creatures. And it is in this latter capacity that we experience energy through awareness.

Awareness, just what is it? Essentially, it is our conscious experience of being and, as such, it also involves the mind. Yet it does so in a way that is so natural as to seem alien to us, especially those of us who have a Western upbringing. To us the mind has acquired a life of its own. We use it to consider matters, as though it is a tool which is external to us rather than an integral part of our being. So divorced from us has our mind become that it is even capable of drawing our attention away from our life as beings interacting with other beings. How often do we not find ourselves – while sitting, standing or walking besides our partner, child, horse or dog, let alone while on our own – preoccupied with matters that are so utterly distant from where we are and what we are doing, as though we have a mind which seems to be completely alienated from our bodies?

How is it possible to be aware of our life as a being, if our mind has gone absent without leave? It is not. So should we block out our mind? Empty and silence it? Still the mind? There are some who claim that we should. Yet it seems to me that if we humans wish to become fully aware of ourselves as beings, creatures of an earth and universe whose constituent parts are constantly in motion interacting with each other at some point or another, the challenge lies not in quieting the mind but in drawing it back into service to ourselves. Yes, the mind is a great intellectual and analytical tool but when it begins to dictate the kind of life we lead, it becomes very much a tail that is trying to wag the dog. And if it is, then it is time for the dog to wag the tail again and for us to reassert control over our mind, not by docking it but rather by harnessing it in our efforts to become conscious humans, being who we are and aware of being so.

This we can do by first of all by focusing our mind on our body, becoming aware of its condition and helping it relax one part at a time. Once we have done this, we can direct our mind to use our senses to explore our immediate surroundings and the earth we stand on, until we are aware of our body as an integral part of that environment and the ground beneath our feet. When our mind becomes one with our body in this ongoing process and awareness of being, we will be in the moment that is always now: being. Yet, however much it may sound like it, the goal of becoming a conscious being is not some impractical, abstract pie-in-the-sky quest. It is a reality that you can learn to achieve through a simple exercise and, if you do it often enough, eventually at the drop of a hat, as it were.

Towards the power of being

Here I could start with an explanation of what I mean but, assuming that actions speak louder than words, as the familiar cliché insists, perhaps it is wiser to start with just such an action. So let me invite you to experience a fraction of the power of being first-hand. It all starts with the very foundation of life as we know it, with breathing and the ground we earthlings so rely on. It does not get more basic than this. And so we return to the earth and the air to find our core. Some call this process "centring". I prefer the term, "grounding", as it embodies both the firmness of the earth and the process of connecting or reconnecting to it and ultimately, through it to ourselves, the very core of our being. It is both a simple process but simultaneously a very demanding one, at least initially, for it requires that we harness the mind and return to the fundamental condition of simply being, with the mind restored to its primary task of nurturing awareness of this ongoing process.

Divorced from the flesh as a result of the extreme limitations of our educational system and our alienation from both self and nature, thought has come to live a life of its own within our body, asserting its control and influence over all that we do and feel. The dominance of thought over our bodies is perhaps most graphically illustrated in the way we allow the past and the future to prevent us from being fully present in the constant here and now. Past regrets and future fears cloud our sense of self in the present. The act of grounding is designed to allow us to reunite the mind with the body, to restore consciousness through all of our senses and to reunite feeling and thought in an experiential presence. And so we become again not a body dominating the mind or thought overriding the flesh but a being that is whole and aware of both itself and its immediate surroundings, authentic and congruent.

But let us experience it rather than merely talk about it. In the next minute you may take an initial step towards the intoxicating power of being by simply following these simple directions. And I would strongly urge you not to skip this section to read further. Instead, I would encourage you to follow the few simple steps below to experience just a very small part of the power of being, for it is only then that you will really begin to understand the words on these pages. Without such understanding, they are only words.

The ground position
The process of grounding starts with the ground position. It is designed to help you relax your body while simultaneously focusing your energy as you connect your body, the earth beneath your feet and your immediate surroundings. To assume the ground position stand upright with your knees slightly bent. Spread your legs until your feet are roughly as far apart as the breadth of your shoulders and tilt your body slightly forward if you need to in order to ensure that it is straight. Shift your contact with the ground more

emphatically to the balls of your feet. If possible and necessary, stand sideways before a mirror to check that your body is straight. Now place your hands on your hips and swivel the base of your pelvis forward and upward. In purely physical terms your body is now capable of moving in any direction at the drop of a hat, much like a horse. In time you will also learn to direct your energy accordingly, so as to be alert and responsive to every demand for movement, even more like a horse.

Being in the moment
To experience the power of being, even if ever so briefly, we also need to enter the moment in which living creatures, such as the horse, truly live their lives: the here and now. Some humans spend their lives trying to live like this all of the time. Conscious, they strive to be fully aware of themselves and their immediate surroundings continuously, just like the horse. Most of us have huge difficulties doing this for any length of time. No wonder other living creatures have difficulties understanding us. What follows is a quick and dirty way of moving into the moment at the drop of a hat. Let us try it before seeking to understand how it works. Just follow the steps. If you do this exercise properly, you will be fully in the moment by the end of it.

Steps to enter into the present moment:
1. Assume the ground position.
2. Breathe slowly and consciously and, as you do, try and lower the location of your breathing from your chest to your belly. Try to relax your abdomen when you do this.
3. Once you manage to do this, focus your awareness on your head. Is it relaxed? Is there any area of tension within it? If there is, focus on that area and consciously seek to relax it before moving on to your neck and doing the same. Once your neck is relaxed, move on to your shoulders and repeat the process. Then go to the next part of your body and do the same, and so on until you

reach your feet and you are aware of your entire body and are relaxed.

4. Now focus your attention on your connection to the earth. Your body is an extension of the earth. You are rooted to it, grounded.
5. While retaining this awareness of your body and its connection to the earth, extend it to include your immediate surroundings, using all of your senses where possible.
6. Now, as you sense yourself and your surroundings, try and feel into what you are sensing, so that you become what you are aware of. Do not try to analyse it but simply accept and appreciate it for what it is, for this is your authentic, conscious energy.

If you have done this correctly, you should end up in a position which resembles how you would sit on a horse with all your energy focused in your core (in your abdomen about a hand's width below your belly button) and your upper body entirely relaxed. More importantly, you will be aware of nothing but your body and your immediate surroundings so acutely that to all intents and purposes you *are* what you are aware of. You will be entirely relaxed and whenever anything occurs, either inside your body or in your immediate surroundings, it will immediately register its presence as a phenomenon of which you are conscious. Yet it will do so not as a stimulus that seems to come from afar but rather as a sense that is part and parcel of the awareness that you have become. And once you are conscious of it, you may choose to focus on it or not.

What this means is that you will be so immersed in the immediacy of every moment, that your mind will not have an opportunity to wonder, for it will not merely be entirely engaged in regulating your awareness of yourself and your surroundings, it will also be part of that consciousness that you have become. You will not have any capacity available for irrelevant thought. And because it is thought, and only thought, that has the ability to generate doubt, fear, regret and all other adverse feelings in the absence of any immediate catastrophe, annoyance or other negative influence, you will find yourself free of those sensations thanks to the banishment of thought. All that you are capable of experiencing in the form of the consciousness that you have become is an overwhelming sense of well-being and calm contentment. It is now that other living creatures, such as the horse, will feel free to come to you. How do I know this? Because this is what our horses have shown me and continue to do so every single day.

In the unlikely event that you have not experienced this sense of well-being and calm contentment after performing this exercise and you feel capable of putting any negative influence aside for the brief period of time involved, why not try it again? But this time try and focus all your energy as you go, from the top of your head to the tips of your toes and then including your immediate surroundings. If it still does not work, there is clearly something really bothering you. This is probably as good a reason as any to read the rest of what I have written, for I have been where you are along the path from there to here and, as I have moved forward, I have drawn many lessons from the horses.

The power of being

Assuming that the exercise has worked for you and you have arrived at the cusp of being and an intense awareness of it, consider for a moment just what this state of conscious being involves. Every single part of us, including our often wayward mind, is involved in being and in being aware of being. As such we are alert and attentive to everything which occurs within us and our immediate surroundings. This means that we are capable of responding and initiating in an instant. And because our mind is so involved in its role of conscious monitor and assessor of being, it has little or no capacity available for a rational assessment of any stimulus followed by the process of devising a response and then implementing it. Instead we are more likely to respond intuitively in the moment, spontaneously drawing on all the physical and mental resources that we have at our disposal. And this likelihood is heightened by the fact that the mind is so preoccupied with conscious living that there is no room for doubt, fear or a considered assessment of eventualities (what-if scenarios, if you like). Instead, the only constant is being.

Sixth sense

It is in this state of total awareness that we are now open to one of the greatest, relatively unexplored and largely undeveloped gifts that we have at our disposal. I am referring to our ability to sense energy, our own and that of others, to influence and be influenced by other sources of energy, especially those of living creatures such as the horse, and to do all of this consciously and intuitively.

If at this stage you are beginning to wonder whether I am not edging too far towards the mystical realm of the fairies, stop and consider your own experience and perhaps what you may have even encountered in popular media reports on scientific research. Who, for instance, has not heard of communication between humans being largely non-verbal? We may listen to someone speaking but how we respond is predominantly determined by our sense of them and how they communicate, and not so much what they say. Alternatively, you may find yourself in a situation in which your mind suggests a logical response but your "gut" prompts you to do the opposite. What about the times when you have instinctively known that a close friend is about to arrive or call and they do? Or when you sense the presence of someone well before your physical senses confirm this?

All of these are examples of heightened awareness which seem to be inexplicable coincidences. Yet they occur so often that it beggars belief to consider them as mere examples of chance occurrences. Indeed, they are so frequent that we have also invented a term to describe the faculty within us which is capable of experiencing such heightened awareness. We half-jokingly refer to it as our "sixth sense". Yet what if it is not a joke or even half of one? What if we do have a sixth sense? What if it is one which we can explore, and even develop, nurture and use?

The good news is that we do, we can and it is not a joke. What our sixth sense detects is energy in some form or another, yes the very thing which Einstein claims is found in everything that has mass. But do not believe me. Consider your own experiences of this sixth sense. Speak to others and listen to theirs. Still not convinced? If you have access to a herd of horses, spend some time watching them communicate. We have learned that certain subtle movements mean certain things but do they really on their own? For instance, you are probably aware that when a horse moves its ears back, it may be giving a warning. Yet horses do the very same thing when they doze. Clearly the same sign has not only different but opposite meanings. So how do we know which one applies? The energy behind it, surely? But let me play devil's advocate. It could be the context in which it occurs rather than the energy behind it, couldn't it? After all, the dozing horse is calm, while the creature flashing a warning is strident. Yet is this not indicative of the energy behind the sign? After all, if the horse flashing a warning was not strident but instead exhibited the energy of dozing within the context of warning, would anyone really take that warning seriously?

It is often claimed that in order to communicate with horses, we need to interact with them, as they do with each other in the wild. In particular, we need to show them that we are their leader and to learn their body language so that we can use it to communicate with them. This approach is based on three assumptions, the first being that horses do this with each other in the wild, the second being that some horses act as leaders and the third that they communicate with each other using no more than body language, meaning that we need to learn to do the same, to communicate with them as horses do.

The problem with this approach is that all three assumptions are false. The horse's primary concern is to feel safe, secure and comfortable, preferably with creatures whom they know, namely, other members of their species. The closest examples of leaders in popular horse culture are the "lead" mare, whom we are usually told is an older experienced member of the herd who responds first to any sign of danger and "leads" the other horses to safety, and the stallion who keeps the group together, rounding up stragglers and chasing off competitors. Of course, if we examine matters more closely, we realise that the "lead" mare, if there is one, does not guide anyone to safety but merely moves to a place they feel is secure and the other horses follow, and that some mares choose to abandon even the fiercest stallion in favour of a rival. Even the stallions choose to keep their harem bands with the herd and in this sense also follow. Put another way, horses are not leaders but followers in that they choose to follow rather than to lead, and the path they follow is that of safety, security and comfort, preferably with their own kind and, if possible, a friend (the intense bonding of pairs of horses is legendary, as is the closeness of a harem band). Are we humans much different in this respect? And if a human is capable of offering safety, security and comfort, what might a horse choose to do?

The assumption that the horse communicates using no more than body language is one that I have already shown to be false. After all, the energy with which the horse uses their body to communicate is equally essential, if not more so. How do we know this? Because there are times when a horse need not even move its ears back to issue a warning. A look may be enough. We know this too from our observations of horses. Again though, it is the energy that is communicated through the eyes, which "speaks", as it were.

So does the horse – or any other species for that matter – really want us to act like another of their kind and try to communicate with them in the same way? Can we really fool the horse that we are also equines by trying to act as a member of their species? Or does the horse decline to ask anything of us, simply leaving it up to us to find a way to them as the kind of creature whom we exactly are ... human ... being ... human? And if we find the way to being human, to fully being the authentic, congruent human that we are capable of becoming, could we learn to exploit our sixth sense in the way that horses do?

Some of the ancient civilizations of Asia teach us humans that we are capable of controlling our energy in the moment, and by doing so, of influencing ourselves and those around us. Slowly, this knowledge is beginning to filter into the world of horses. Mark Rashid has introduced it through his practice of Aikido. Klaus

Ferdinand Hempfling has implemented it in his body and spiritual awareness exercises, an influence taken up and amplified by some of his former students. Michael Bevilacqua and Linda Kohanov have shared it with us through their insightful writings. Increasingly, a growing number of us are taking what we have learned from Tai Chi Chuan (Taijiquan) and Chi Kung (Qigong), and are implementing it in our daily lives and interaction with our horses. Humans throughout the horse world are beginning to discover the power of being and its potential for improving their lives, those of their horses and the interaction between the species, especially when the mix is extended to include calm, patience, intent, flexibility and pliant strength.

This is a movement that is still in its infancy. Yet it is one which holds great promise. And this promise is not something that is far-removed like the light at the end of the tunnel. It is here to be plucked and relished at any time of our choosing. We can start on this journey whenever we want to and enjoy some of its benefits almost immediately, if we have not yet already done so. The first step is to assume the ground position. The second you already know. We are embarked on the path to the horse and ultimately to the human whom we are capable of becoming through the power of being.

EPILOGUE

And so we come full circle to living what was merely an intellectual understanding at the start of the journey initiated in the first article of this book but is now a way of life:

> Let us put ambition to one side and begin to listen and to see. Above all, let us begin to "feel"! The ability to feel is a gift from God to each of us. Let us begin to feel ourselves and to understand our horses. Let us commit ourselves to this journey which is attended by unending successes and constant joy, this journey that makes it possible for us to stop putting off enjoyment of today's work until tomorrow, or the day after, or until we have achieved some goal of questionable worth. Let us begin this journey that allows us *to live fully in the here and now*, just as our horses actually teach us to do.
>
> (Klaus Ferdinand Hempfling, *Dancing with Horses*, p. 19 – emphasis added).

AN INVITATION…

If you have found this book worth reading and are in agreement with the approach towards horses which it advocates, may I invite you to leave a positive review on the website of the retailer where you purchased it. The more positive reviews there are, the more likely it is to be read by other humans who are looking for a more horse-friendly way of being with their horses.

ALSO AVAILABLE

A large part of the journey which has resulted in the publication of this book is documented in a series of three books entitled *In Search of the Master Who Dances with Horses: Challenge*, *Growth* and *Being*. The blurb is as follows.

> Based on social media statistics, Klaus Ferdinand Hempfling is arguably the most popular horse trainer in the world, with far more likes on Facebook and views on YouTube than any other horseman on the planet. At a certain point in time he invited people to join him as part of a very small select group to study with him full-time for a year.
>
> Urgently in need of a meaningful change of life, a man decides to cross the world together with his wife, a horse and a dog to be part of that small select group of people. He too would like to learn how to dance with horses. Perhaps it will then also be possible for him to teach others to do the same one day.
>
> This book documents the man's reflections from the time he starts to prepare for his life-changing experience. Join him in his discovery and appreciation of some of the work being done not only of the master who dances with horses but also of other great horse people, such as Michael Bevilacqua, the main international representative of Nevzorov Haute Ecole, Linda Kohanov, Frédéric Pignon, Mark Rashid, Stormy May, Carolyn Resnick and Chuck Mintzlaff. Accompany him as he travels across Europe to find the truth about horses and humans which he is seeking. And watch as he begins to discover where that truth really lies.

You can find out where to buy the first of these books by visiting the Books page of the Horses and Humans website at http://www.horsesandhumans.com/mainsite/challenge.htm.

FEEL FREE TO CONTACT ME

Feedback is welcome. You may email me at liamsga@gmail.com or contact me through my Facebook page at https://www.facebook.com/andrewglynsmail.

Horses and Humans also has a publications page on Facebook at https://www.facebook.com/horsesandhumans and a group page at https://www.facebook.com/groups/horsesandhumans/. Please feel free to join the Horses and Humans group and make a contribution to helping people become the kind of human a horse seeks to be with. The Horses and Humans blog may be found at www.horsesandhumans.com/blog/.

BIBLIOGRAPHY AND OTHER RESOURCES

Here I would like to leave you with the references to those which I deem to be a vital part of my library. I have broken them down into two lists: *Essential* and *Recommended Resources*. All of the resources are books except where otherwise noted.

Essential books and other resources
Beck, Andy, *Horsonality*, e-book available at http://www.equine-behavior.com/Downloads/ppp.htm

Bevilacqua, Michael, *Beyond the Dream Horse: A Revealing Perspective on Attaining a True Relationship*, Equi-Forme, Quebec, 2010 (www.beyondthedreamhorse.ca)

– *Au-delà du Cheval de Rêve: Comment créer une relation authentique avec votre cheval*, Equi-Forme, Quebec, 2010 (www.beyondthedreamhorse.ca)

– *Freunde Fürs Leben: Ehrliche Partnerschaft Mit Deinem Pferd*, Equi-Forme, Quebec, 2010 (www.beyondthedreamhorse.ca)

Kathrens, Ginger, *Cloud: The Wild Stallion of the Rockies Collection*, Australian Broadcasting Corporation, 2011, (www.abcshop.com.au). The three documentaries on this DVD are also available free of charge to viewers in North America at www.pbs.org.

May, Stormy, *The Path of the Horse: Taking the First Step* (DVD), Stormy May Productions, 2008 (now available free on YouTube at https://www.youtube.com/watch?v=TQUMAJCh1fA)

Tolle, Eckhart, *The Power of Now: A Guide to Spiritual Enlightenment*, Hachette Australia, Sydney, 2004

– *Practising the Power of Now: A Guide to Spiritual Enlightenment*, Hodder & Stoughton, London, 2011

A Tai Chi or Feldenkrais course with reference materials (video and/or book) that you can take home with you.

Recommended books and resources

Barclay, Harold, *The Role of the Horse in Man's Culture*, J.A. Allen, London, 1980

Bowe, Andrew, *The Barefoot Blacksmith: Vol. 2. Maintenance Trimming*, The Barefoot Blacksmith, 2007 (www.barehoofcare.com)

Budras, K., Sack, W.O. and Röck, S, *Anatomy of the Horse*, Schlütersche, Hannover, 2011

Clayton, H.M., Flood, P.F. and Rosenstein, D.S., *Clinical Anatomy of the Horse*, Mosby Elsevier, Edinburgh, 2005

Delgado, Magali and Pignon, Frédéric with Walser, David, *Gallop to Freedom: Training Horses with Our Six Golden Principles*, Trafalgar Square, North Pomfret, 2009

Hempfling, Klaus Ferdinand, *Coming Together* (DVD), J.A. Allen, London, 2005

– *Dancing with Horses: Collected Riding on a Loose Rein* (book), Trafalgar Square, North Pomfret, 2001

– *Dancing with Horses* (DVD), J.A. Allen, London, 1999

– *De Boodschap van de Paarden*, Uitgeverij Karnak, Amsterdam, 2002

– *Die Botschaft der Pferde*, Goldmann, 1998

– *The Horse Seeks Me*, Cadmos, London, 2010

Higgins, Gillian, *How Your Horse Moves: A Unique Visual Guide to Improving Performance*, David and Charles, Newton Abbot, 2011

– *Horses Inside Out: Movement from the Anatomical Perspective* (DVD), 2009, (www.horsesinsideout.com)

Kohanov, Linda, *The Tao of Equus: A Woman's Journey of Healing and Transformation through the Way of the Horse*, New World Library, Novato, 2001

May, Stormy, *The Path of the Horse: From Competition to Compassion*, Our Horses Press, 2012 (www.ourhorses.org)

Nevzorov, Alexander, *Nevzorov Haute Ecole Principles* (DVD), Nevzorov Haute École, 2006, (www.hauteecole.ru)

– *The Horse Crucified and Risen*, Nevzorov Haute École, Charlestown, 2011 (www.hauteecole.ru)

– *The Horse Crucified and Risen: Parts I and II* (DVD), Nevzorov Haute École, (www.hauteecole.ru)

– *Tractate on a School Mount*, Nevzorov Haute École, Nevzorov Haute École, Charlestown, 2011 (www.hauteecole.ru)

Rashid, Mark, *Horses Never Lie: The Heart of Passive Leadership*, David & Charles, Cincinnati, 2000

Resnick, Carolyn, *Naked Liberty: Memoirs of My Childhood*, Amigo Publications, Los Olivos, 2005

– *Introduction to the Waterhole Rituals* (DVD), Stormy May Productions, 2008, (www.carolynresnick.com)

Ruddock, Jock, *The Equine Touch: From Zero to Hero in Your Horse's Eyes*, The Equine Touch Foundation, 2008 (www.theequinetouch.com)

Spilker, Imke, *Empowered Horses*, Trafalgar Square, North Pomfret, 2009

Veldman, Frans and Kooistra, Ilona, *Hoef Natuurlijk: Gezondere Hoeven en Betere Prestaties in Sport en Recreatie*, Paard Natuurlijk, Netherlands, 2007 (www.hoefnatuurlijk.nl)

– *Natuurlijk Bekappen* (DVD), Paard Natuurlijk, Netherlands, 2005 (www.paardnatuurlijk.nl)

– *Paard Natuurlijk: Gezondere Paarden en Betere Prestaties in Sport en Recreatie*, Paard Natuurlijk, Netherlands, 2010 (www.paardnatuurlijk.nl)

Wing-Ming, Yang, *Tai Chi Chuan: Classical Yang Style*, Second Edition (book), YMAA Publication Centre, Wolfeboro, 2010 (www.ymaa.com)

– Yang, *Tai Chi Chuan: Classical Yang Style*, Second Edition (DVD), YMAA Publication Centre, Wolfeboro, 2010 (www.ymaa.com)

www.ingramcontent.com/pod-product-compliance
Lightning Source LLC
LaVergne TN
LVHW051234080426
835513LV00016B/1586